Contents

INTRODUCTION /*vii*

PART ONE: TECHNICAL HINTS / *1*

PART TWO: RECIPES / *65*

SECTION ONE: GRAPE WINES / *67*

SECTION TWO: OTHER CONCENTRATES / *79*

SECTION THREE: COUNTRY WINES / *87*

SECTION FOUR: LIQUEURS / *100*

SECTION FIVE: SECOND WINES / *104*

SECTION SIX: FUN AND FRIVOLITY WITH WINE /*108*

SECTION SEVEN: TWELVE-DAY WINES, OR POP
WINES / *112*

APPENDIX: METRIC SYSTEM / *117*

For the late Barbara Milligan

Introduction

This book introduces a revolutionary process for the home winemaker—*wines ready to drink in 10 to 15 days from the date you start fermentation*! You can send out the invitations to a party, and then start to make the wine you will serve—from 1 to 5 gallons at a batch.

This type of wine is ideal for the apartment dweller, or anyone else who has not the space to make and store large quantities of traditional wines; it is ideal for people who are going to move in three months, and therefore cannot put down wine to age in the cellar.

These 15-day wines—"pop wines" as they're sometimes called—are not intended to replace the traditional wines made by those who have the necessary facilities to produce and mature them, and the palate to enjoy them. We give in this book many recipes for such high-quality wines.

This is not a book for beginners. It is written for people who already understand the basic winemaking process, and who have had some practical experience of making wine at home.

If you are just starting to make wine, or if you want to give a book to someone else who is just starting, you should choose *The Art of Making Wine* by the same authors. That book explains, in detail, all you need to know to choose equipment and materials, and to make a number of different wines.

This volume does not repeat all the basic material. Part I contains technical information that will be helpful to experienced winemakers.

Part II contains wine recipes. Many of these were developed in the Wine-Art research centre in Vancouver, Canada. All the wines described here have been made, properly matured, taste-tested, and proven to be winners.

The recipes include a number of grape wines; and there are wines made from concentrates of other fruits besides the grape. There is also a collection of "country wines" made from garden fruits and vegetables, and from wild fruits and berries.

We give a group of recipes for the 15-day "pop" wines, plus general instructions on creating your own recipes for these wines.

I would like to put on record that much of the research that preceded the writing of this book was done by Barbara Milligan, of Vancouver, B.C. Her skill and enthusiasm contributed greatly to making these recipes and working instructions so varied and helpful.

Try these recipes! With some, you'll be fascinated by the ease and speed of processing; and with all of them you'll enjoy the flavour and aroma of the finished wines.

PART ONE

Technical
Hints

The word "wine", unqualified, means the fermented juice of the grape, *vitis vinifena*. Under ideal conditions, the only modification needed is to add 100 parts per million of the preservative sulphur dioxide, most of which is dissipated before the wine is consumed.

Note the phrase "under ideal conditions". Those conditions would include an adequate supply of a superlative grape variety from a perfect vintage year. Unfortunately, such conditions do not recur often enough to supply one-tenth of the world's wine requirements; therefore, nature usually needs a little assistance from the helping hand of man.

That means balancing the proportions of sugar, acids, minerals, vitamins and enzymes in the must; it means maintaining and using pure yeast strains. With care, these procedures will yield for us, every year, an abundance of good wine and, sometimes, a moderate supply of great wine.

Some purists object to this tinkering with nature; yet I notice that these people seldom object to the efforts of the doctor and nutritionist to keep them healthy! For my part, I see little difference; good bodily health and good wine both need intelligent forethought and a modicum of continued skilled care.

During the last decade or two, home winemakers have become more and more efficient in carrying out these procedures. Two influences, I think, have produced this development.

FIRST: many people have developed a discriminating palate for wine; they won't themselves drink inferior wines, and they won't serve such rubbish to their families and friends.

SECOND: the technical knowledge of commercial enologists, formerly kept secret by the people who made a living from it, has become widely available in print, adapted so as to be applicable by the home winemaker.

So far as I know, the first such book was *American Wines and Wine-making*, by Philip Wagner, published in 1935. It has been revised several times, and is still an excellent text on the processing of fresh grapes.

The next major writer in this field was Mrs. S.M. Tritton, M.P.S., F.R.I.C. Her book *Amateur Winemaking* covers not only grapes, but many other domestic and wild fruits, too. Originally written for the English market, this book has been revised and now includes American and metric measurements. All of Mrs. Tritton's recipes, if carefully followed, yield excellent wine.

There are other good winemaking books available, of course; but Wagner and Tritton must have credit as pioneers who prepared the way for the later researchers and writers in this field.

There is no need, in a book like this, for a step-by-step

explanation of winemaking procedures. Therefore this part of the book lists alphabetically a number of subjects on which the advanced winemaker may occasionally run into difficulties, or may be interested in additional technical information.

ACID BLENDS

There has been some debate over the ideal composition of the acid blends used for correcting low acid levels in the must. Here I discuss the merits and demerits of the acids most commonly used.

But first, one important practical point: all acids should be dissolved in water before you add them to the must, then thoroughly stirred in; this will ensure even distribution, and accuracy of the subsequent acid testing.

CITRIC ACID / Citric acid has the advantage that it tends to remove any metal contamination (*e.g.*, minute traces of iron or copper from the winemaking equipment), also that it is not easily precipitated in the wine. Yet, in my judgment, citric acid does not produce a good vinous flavour.

LACTIC ACID / Some writers on winemaking are enthusiastic about using lactic acid for home-made wines. To be sure, if a finished wine is low in acid, the addition of 2 teaspoons of lactic acid per gallon will improve its flavour or freshness.

Yet lactic acid must be used with discretion; it is a by-product of fermentation, and is not usually present in the fresh grape or other fruit. Too much of it will alter the bouquet of the wine, and make it smell like milk! Because of the importance of bouquet in red wines, I would recommend using lactic acid only in light white wines.

Food-grade lactic acid is a liquid, rather hard to get, and priced at about 45 cents per ounce.

SUCCINIC ACID / Recently it has been suggested that succinic acid is a desirable additive to home-made wines. Certainly it is found in many good, well-aged grape wines, and seems to provide part of the complex, well-balanced flavour. Like lactic acid, it is usually not found in fresh grapes or other fruits; it is a by-product of the fermentation.

Some writers assert that the addition of succinic acid in small quantities is good, but only if the wine is to be kept for 2 years or more.

Bearing in mind that this acid is quite expensive, I would suggest that it is not needed in wine made from fresh grapes; but when you are using other fruits, or grape concentrate, you may care to try very small quantities of succinic acid.

At the time of writing, succinic acid costs about $1 per ounce. If you wish to use it, 1 gram per gallon is sufficient, as part of the total acid addition.

28.35 grams = 1 ounce; so for larger volumes of must, the following weights of succinic acid would be about right:

For 5 gallons must, 1/6 ounce
For 10 gallons must, ⅓ ounce
For 30 gallons must, 1 ounce.

Succinic acid is very difficult to dissolve, so you will have to use hot water.

TARTARIC ACID / Many winemakers feel that the use of tartaric acid produces a softer, more vinous wine in the long run. Therefore I recommend the use of an acid blend that is predominantly tartaric.

ACID CONTENT

Before the advent of modern testing techniques, most home-made wines contained too little acid and, for many palates, were somewhat bland and flavourless. Some winemakers now have gone to the other extreme, with acid levels a bit too high.

For a red table wine, I would suggest an acid content of .65%, unless you intend to keep the wine for 2 to 5 years, in which case an acid level of .7% would probably be desirable.

For a white table wine that is to be drunk fairly young, .7% is adequate; if the wine is to be kept for more than a year or two, .75% is not too much.

Acid content for pop wines should be low, because they are going to be drunk while still quite new; .5% is ample.

With fruit wines, if you depend solely on testing the acid level of the unfermented must, it's easy to end up with considerable excess acid. Let's examine the cause of this problem, and see how to avoid it.

Commercial wineries, and home winemakers, using fresh grapes or grape concentrate, find that the acid level declines during fermentation: some tartaric acid is converted to cream of tartar, and precipitated; some malic acid is converted to the softer lactic acid.

Fruit wines are different. My experience in many tests shows that you are not likely to have any measurable decline of acid levels during fermentation. Indeed, if you are fermenting on the fruit – as with fresh cherries, plums or apricots – there will be a considerable *increase* of acid content, as the newly formed alcohol extracts acid from the skins and pulp. This extraction will be about 1.5 parts of acid per thousand.

So you should take this into account when preparing the must. For fresh fruits that are to be fermented on the pulp, start with a total acid level of .5%; you can safely predict that it will increase to .6% or .65% by the time you remove the fruit from the must. For a fruit wine, that's about right.

ACID TESTING

Acid content is measured by an acid testing kit. Full instructions were given in *The Art of Making Wine*. In brief, this is the method:

1/ To a measured sample (15 cc. is usually enough) of must or wine, add an indicating liquid, phenolphthalein, that is clear in an acid solution, pink in a neutral or alkaline solution.

2/ Slowly add measured amounts of alkali (sodium hydroxide, *i.e.* caustic soda) that will neutralize the fruit acids.

3/ When the phenolphthalein changes colour, you know that all the acid has been neutralized. The amount of alkali you have used is precisely proportional to the amount of acid that was present in the first place.

It's basically simple, but a few problems do arise from time to time:

a/ I said above that the colour change of phenolphthalein at neutralization is from clear to pink. But that effect is sometimes masked by the colour or chemical composition of the sample under test.

The safe rule is to keep watching for *any* distinct, permanent colour change; that is the correct end point. If you keep adding more and more alkali, trying to achieve a bright pink coloration, you may get misleading results from your test.

For instance, if a red wine turns gray, that's the signal to stop. Another red wine might turn green; blue-red may turn to blue-gray; a white wine may show just a tinge of grayish pink.

b/ Another problem springs from the increasing number of winemakers' supply firms. Different strengths of sodium hydroxide solution are being sold for acid testing.

I opted for the testing system developed by Philip Wagner, which uses sodium hydroxide of the strength designated as 1/5 normal. A major advantage of using this solution is that, in a 15 cc. wine sample, 1 cc. of the alkali will neutralize 1 part per thousand of acid. So you get the result of your test with no calculations.

Many laboratories employ similar methods to test acids in liquids other than wine; some of them use alkali only 1/10 normal – half the strength that I recommend.

Some people who go into the winemakers' supply business don't understand the chemistry of acid testing; some, who do understand, simply won't contract to have a standardized product made for them. The result is that some stores sell 1/10 normal alkali solution for acid testing. If you use this solution without knowing its strength, your test results will all be wrong.

So when you buy an acid testing kit with sodium hydroxide solution included, or when you buy refills, ask what is the strength. If there's a choice, take the 1/5 normal. If you have to accept the 1/10 normal solution, you can make the test as usual but, to find the parts acid per thousand, *divide the terminal number by 2*. That's because the 1/10 normal solution is half the strength of the 1/5 normal; so it takes 2 cc. of 1/10 normal to neutralize the same amount of acid as 1 cc. of 1/5 normal.

For example: if it takes 8 cc. of 1/5 normal sodium hydroxide to produce a colour change, then the wine contains 8 parts acid per thousand (.8%).

The same wine would require 16 cc. of 1/10 normal sodium hydroxide to produce the colour change. So the acid content is $\frac{16}{2} = 8$ parts per thousand (.8%).

c/Some people have trouble in recognizing the colour change; they would not normally be called colour-blind, yet their eyes just don't detect minute colour changes in a sample of wine. The difficulty occurs especially with blue-red fruit, where the strong colour of the juice tends to mask the colour of the phenolphthalein at neutralization point.

The remedy: measure out the usual 15 cc. sample of juice; then, before beginning the test, dilute it about 10 to 1 with distilled water. You need not measure the water exactly; you are still going to test only the amount of acid in that 15 cc. of must or wine. Just make sure that the water is thoroughly stirred in; the mixture is now a much paler colour than was the undiluted sample, so you will find that it's much easier to see the colour change when it occurs.

Add the alkali just as before, watch for the colour change and take the reading just as you would for undiluted wine or must. I emphasize that no multiplication, division or other calculation is required to compensate for the dilution.

(One precaution: it's essential to use distilled water. Acids or alkalis in ordinary tap water could seriously affect the test results.)

Another helpful method, in cases where you have trouble detecting the colour change: use two identical vials and put 15 cc. of the must or wine in each. Make the test only on vial number 1. Vial number 2, the untreated one, serves as the norm; by comparing the two, you can more easily check the colour change in vial number 1.

ACID TESTING-ANOTHER METHOD / The Ames Company, who make Dextro Check for measuring residual sugar in finished wines, have now developed Mustix, a product for measuring acid content of unfermented must. You dip a strip of specially treated paper in the must, and it changes colour. You compare this colour change to a chart supplied with each package of strips, and immediately read off the acid content.

There are seven colours to be matched, ranging from blue through green to yellow; these indicate acid content from zero up to 12 parts per thousand acid as tartaric. The graduations on the scale, in parts per thousand, are 0, 1.5, 3, 5, 7, 9 and 12 (*i.e.*, 0%, .15%, .3%, .5%, .7%, .9% and 1.2%).

The manufacturers suggest that, to get more accurate values, you should be able to interpolate readings between the graduations, say between 5 and 7 or 7 and 9 parts per thousand. My research staff found this impossible; even with a mixture of acid and water, we could not get closer than 2 parts per thousand. This is not nearly so accurate as the ordinary acid testing procedure with sodium hydroxide and phenolphthalein which, with care, will give readings of total acid to ½ part per thousand.

I would say, then, that Mustix is quick and easy to use, but gives only a rough measurement of acid content. Another drawback: it won't measure acid in wine, because the Mustix reaction doesn't work in the presence of alcohol.

ADDITIVES

There has been growing public concern in recent years about the flavouring, colouring and preservative substances being added to foods and beverages to stabilize them or to improve their taste and appearance. Let's take a look at the various additives used by the home winemaker.

First, consider what may be called the organic additives, substances that occur naturally in fruits and vegetables.

SUGARS / In all wine-yielding fruits and vegetables, sugar is the fermentable ingredient that produces the alcohol. Well-ripened wine grapes contain enough sugar to make a satisfying, stable wine; unfortunately some grapes, and most of the other fruits and vegetables we use, have an inadequate sugar content. So, to get good wine, we add sugar: cane sugar, corn sugar (dextrose) or fruit sugar (levulose).

ACIDS / Citric, tartaric, malic, succinic and lactic acids all occur naturally in grape juice; sorbic acid is not often found in grapes, but is present in many other fruits.

Yet some grapes, and some other fruits, do not contain the quantities or proportions of acid that would produce an ideal invironment for the fermenting yeast, or yield the desired flavour in the finished wine. So we improve the acid content by adding individual acids, or a suitable acid blend, to the must.

YEAST ENERGIZER / Vitamins B and C, plus protein derived from soya beans, are the principal ingredients of yeast energizer (one trade name is Vita-Vin). The vitamins, and the nitrogen of the bean protein, stimulate the growth of the yeast and so make the fermentation more vigorous.

Vitamin B is found in the germ and bran of all the food grains, and is an important ingredient in many health breads and health cereals.

Vitamin C, or ascorbic acid, is present in most fruits and vegetables; a regular supply of this vitamin is essential to good health.

SODIUM ERYTHORBATE/I group this with the organic additives because it is an isomer of vitamin C. For a full description of its uses, see "Antioxidants", page 14

GRAPE TANNIN/Tannin is present in many trees and plants – in oak-galls and tea-leaves, for example. As winemakers, we are concerned with the tannin content of grape stems and seeds. In the proper quantities, this imparts a pleasing tang or bite to the finished wine. (The tannin flavour may be too strong in new wine; but it softens and mellows as the wine matures.)

But the problem is that some fruits are deficient in tannin; so if your palate is accustomed to the authentic tannin flavour, you will find a low-tannin or no-tannin wine too bland and smooth. The remedy: add an appropriate quantity of grape tannin. The recipes in Part II indicate where this should be done.

MAGNESIUM SULPHATE, UREA, AMMONIUM SULPHATE/These are sources of minerals and nitrogen that are helpful to the vigorous growth of wine yeast. But not all grapes, and not all other fruits, have enough of them. So you add enough of them to stimulate fermentation; they are commonly all added together, under the name "Yeast Nutrient".

When yeast nutrient is required, I would urge that you use the amount in the recipe, and no more. That's not because the ingredients are toxic, but because they have a rather bitter flavour. Used in correct amounts, they are all consumed by the yeast; but if you add excessive amounts, some will be left over, and then your wine will taste bitter.

(With these nutrients, just as with sugar, tannin, etc., enough is enough, and too much will spoil the wine. Similarly, food, drink and exercise are good for the body – in correct amounts. In excess, they may be injurious.)

PECTIC ENZYME/An enzyme is an organic catalyst that speeds, or improves the efficiency of, one of the chemical processes necessary to life. In the human body, for example, the enzyme lipase helps to digest fats; diastase digests starches.

Pectin, which is present in many fruits, is a kind of binding agent. (Its name is derived from a Greek word meaning "to make firm or solid".) Pectin tends to prevent the fruit juice from leaving the pulp during pressing or primary fermentation, and then it tends to hold solids in suspension while the wine is maturing.

Pectic enzyme, or pectinase, digests and removes this pectin, and so yields more juice and more flavour from your fruit, and improves the colour, clarity and flavour of your finished wine.

NATURAL OR SYNTHETIC? / These organic additives can be extracted from fruits and vegetables: for example, the well-known processes for making sugar from cane or beets. Several of them can also be made in the laboratory; but some people would find fault with this, and would assert that only naturally-occurring nutrients should be consumed, as being somehow superior to the others. There is no space here for a full treatment of this controversy. I will just mention a couple of points.

Dr. Linus Pauling confirms, in his book *Vitamin C and the Common Cold*, that the synthetically produced ascorbic acid is exactly as beneficial, for every dietetic and therapeutic purpose, as the naturally occurring form.

Some of the extreme "pure food" advocates even condemn alcohol as an artificially produced, and therefore dangerous, additive to pure fruit juice! This theory can easily be refuted. Alcohol is often formed, without any human intervention, by the natural fermentation of ripe fruit, and many wild creatures enjoy it. One can sometimes see, for example, wild birds in winter eating windfall fruit that has fermented. They get slightly drunk, stagger about on the ground, and perform wild aerobatics in flight; yet they like it so much that they keep coming back for more. If that isn't "natural food" I don't know what is!

Anyone who, on religious or moral grounds, abstains from wine has my full respect; but I firmly reject the theory that alcoholic fermentation is somehow unnatural.

NON-ORGANIC SUBSTANCES

COPPER SULPHATE / We do not add copper sulphate to wine, but it is commonly used in the vineyard as a spray, to prevent mildew on the grapes. Some small amount of it may remain on the grape skins, and so find its way into the must after crushing and pressing. It serves no useful purpose in fermentation; indeed, the less of it there is in the must, the better. However, the copper sulphate treatment has been in use for many years; vintners are well aware of the quantities to apply; and I have never heard of anyone suffering the slightest harm from it.

SULPHUR DIOXIDE / Sulphur dioxide, SO_2, has been used by all wineries in the world for well over half a century. It serves as a sterilant, to eliminate spoilage organisms from the must, and so leave a clear field for the working of the selected wine yeast. This procedure is absolutely essential if you want to get good wine every time. Sulphur dioxide is also used in small quantities at later stages of the winemaking process as an anti-oxidant. (See "Antioxidants", page 24).

Sulphur dioxide is just about perfect for these purposes. The only possible drawback to its use is that, *in excess*, it produces a noticeable bad smell and taste. Government-imposed limits on SO_2 content vary somewhat in different countries, but generally the permissible maximum content of free sulphur dioxide runs from 300 to 400 parts per million. This level would be physically harmless, but I'm sure the smell and taste would make the wine undrinkable. Most commercially made wines, when they reach the consumer, contain about 20 to 50 p.p.m. SO_2, and one seldom hears any complaints about smell or flavour at that level.

So here are some general guidelines. In the fresh must, use a maximum of 200 parts per million SO_2; most or all of that will be lost during fermentation. Prior to final bottling, use not more than 50 p.p.m. Much of this will disappear as the wine ages; you will end up with 10 to 20 p.p.m. in the matured wine; and there is not the slightest fear that this amount will be detectable by taste buds or nose, or that it will injure your health.

The most convenient sources of sulphur dioxide for home winemaking are potassium metabisulphite and sodium metabisulphite, used as loose crystals or as the 7-grain Campden tablets.

What about the effect of the metabisulphite itself?

"O.K., so it tastes like brimstone and fire. Relax, we'll add molasses and serve it as spring tonic."

Campden tablets have long been used in the home bottling of fruit; yet neither in this process, nor in home winemaking, are there any reports of harm caused by the use of metabisulphite.

It has been noted that ingestion of metabisulphite does cause a slight increase in the excretion of calcium. This might, in rare cases, be undesirable: for example, a pregnant woman who is on the borderline of malnutrition needs every scrap of calcium she can retain to nourish the foetus and to protect her own teeth. But if she is eating a medically approved, well-balanced diet, she need not worry about any shortage of calcium from this cause. For some other people, a little extra elimination of calcium could be beneficial; retention of excess calcium in the body has been linked with the appearance of aging in the skin, and with several diseases involving stony deposits in the joints and internal organs.

Metabisulphite also has a slight tendency to destroy thiamin, one of the B vitamins. However, home-made, unfiltered wines, because of the yeast they contain, generally have a higher vitamin B content than commercial wines; this would tend to offset any slight loss of thiamin due to the metabisulphite.

WINE AS NUTRIMENT

Winemaking, in effect, is a process of preserving the food value that nature has put into the fruit. Left alone,

Use a little wine for thy stomach's sake.— I Timothy 5:23

"I have cut down considerably on my consumption, Doctor, and I am well aware that 'a little wine' is not a gallon to the layman—however, it is to the winemaker!"

the grapes, gooseberries or plums will decompose into the ingredients from which the vine, bush or tree originally made them. We winemakers prevent that breakdown, and enjoy the flavour, aroma and appearance of our product.

I am not trying to promote wine as a medicine or as a health food; but I do say confidently that everything you consume in your wine, either from the basic fruits, the yeast, or the recommended additives, would be ingested by anyone who eats a sound, varied diet, including fruit and vegetables. As millions of winemakers know, the moderate use of well-made wines is conducive to human health and happiness.

ALCOHOL CONTENT

Most winemakers are interested in knowing the alcohol content of their wines; unfortunately, you can't measure it by tasting. One item sold to measure alcohol content is the vinometer. It is cheap, but really can't be recommended for accuracy; readings are affected by temperature and by the sugar content of the wine. Moreover, because vinometers are so cheap, some manufacturers show little concern for quality control.

The Art of Making Wine described a method that requires no apparatus except a hydrometer and thermometer, and gives fairly accurate readings for all wines, sweet and dry.

Many wineries use the ebulliometer for alcohol testing; but there has recently become available an instrument that in my opinion is better, the alcohol refractometer.

The refractometer is fairly new to this continent, but it has been widely used in Europe. Significantly, the British Customs and Excise Department accepts refractometer readings of alcohol for taxation purposes.

The refractometer is about the size and shape of a microscope. Its operation depends on the fact that the refractive index of wine varies with its alcohol content. It is not cheap; but it costs no more—sometimes less—than an ebulliometer. It is simpler to use, and is not affected by the sugar content of the wine. As for accuracy, it measures alcohol to within 1/10 of 1%. It uses only a few drops of wine, and takes only about 3 minutes to get a result—faster than an ebulliometer, than distillation, or than the method described in *The Art of Making Wine*.

There are three steps to the process:
1/First measure the specific gravity of the wine. Calculate the difference (we call it D) between the S.G. of the wine and 1.000, the S.G. of pure water. If the S.G. of the wine is less than 1.000, D has a negative value.

E.g., S.G. of a dry table wine = .994

1.000 − .994 = .006

Ignore the decimal point and any zeros in the first or

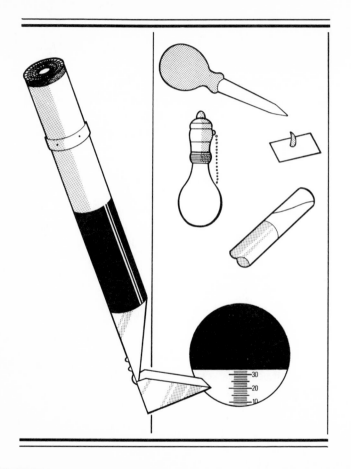

second decimal places, and use only the "units" of this difference figure. Then D = −6

Another example: S.G. of a sweet dessert wine = 1.013
1.013 − 1.00 = .013

So in this case, D = 13

2 / Open the hinged prism-box of the refractometer and, with a rod or a baster, put one or two drops of wine on the lower prism (the one fixed to the eyepiece). Close the prism box again; the wine sample spreads into a thin film between the two prisms. Point the instrument at a light, look through the eyepiece, and if necessary adjust the focus to get a sharp image. You see the field of view divided into light and dark portions. The dividing line between light and dark cuts a numbered scale. The position of this dividing line on the scale indicates the refractive index of the wine. (We call it R.)

3 / Now calculate R − D; look up the resulting figure in the table that comes with the instrument, and instantly read off the alcohol content of the wine.

E.g., take the dry table wine for which D = −6

Suppose R = 36

Then R − D = 42 (Subtracting −6 means *adding* 6)

The table shows alcohol content = 10.1%

Take the dessert wine for which D = 13

The refractometer shows that R = 69.5

Then R − D = 56.5

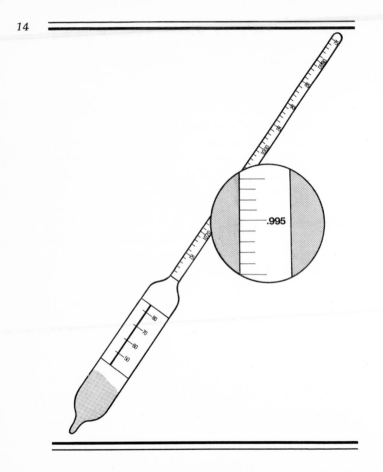

Alcohol content = 15.3%

The main precautions for getting accurate results are:

a / The instrument must be kept scrupulously clean.

b / The wine sample and refractometer must be at the same temperature, or you will get a false reading. If you store the refractometer in the same place as the wine, you'll have no trouble on this score.

You can have your wine supplier bring in an alcohol refractometer from England; full instructions come with the instrument.

The ordinary hydrometer used in wine and beer making is not accurate enough for use with the refractometer; you should get two very accurate narrow-range hydrometers (they cost about $10 each), one reading from .975 to 1.000, the other from 1.000 to 1.025, and a large hydrometer jar.

For the really keen, advanced winemaker, or for a winemakers' club to use as a service to members, this instrument would be an interesting, worthwhile investment.

ANTIOXIDANTS

Oxidation used to be one of the most common problems for home winemakers. The use of the fermentation lock, metabisulphite crystals, and ascorbic acid has done much to reduce oxidation, but it remains a potential hazard, particularly for people who produce wine in large quantities. Here are a few practical hints for minimizing that hazard.

SULPHUR DIOXIDE/The best source of sulphur dioxide for home winemaking is potassium metabisulphite; this is better than sodium metabisulphite because it gives a larger yield of sulphur dioxide (SO_2) and is less likely to be contaminated by heavy metals. For practical purposes you can assume that potassium metabisulphite will yield 50% by weight of SO_2.

Here are some suggested quantities for practical use:
1 teaspoon in 10 U.S. gals. = 60 p.p.m. SO_2
1 teaspoon in 10 Canadian gals. = 50 p.p.m. SO_2
1 ounce in 100 U.S. gals. = 42 p.p.m. SO_2
1 ounce in 100 Canadian gals. = 35 p.p.m. SO_2

(For calculating intermediate quantities, figure that 1 ounce of potassium metabisulphite, in fine granular form, equals 4½ level teaspoons.)

These quantities are fully adequate for sound wine at the time of racking or bottling.

SODIUM ERYTHORBATE/It has been known for some time that ascorbic acid, or vitamin C, present in varying quantities in all fresh fruits, is an antioxidant.

Specially important for winemakers is the fact that SO_2 and ascorbic acid have a synergistic effect—each reinforces the action of the other, so a certain quantity of both will give more antioxidant effect than would the same quantity of either one separately. This lets you use much less SO_2, and still have your wine protected.

The only problem is that ascorbic acid is rather expensive. Fortunately there is available an isomer of ascorbic acid, called sodium erythorbate; it does not have the therapeutic effect of vitamin C, but it is equally non-toxic, it is equally effective as an antioxidant, and it has just the same synergistic effect with SO_2 as does vitamin C. Moreover, sodium erythorbate is cheaper than vitamin C – cheap enough that you can afford to use it for large-scale production of wine.

Sodium erythorbate is available by the ounce, also in 7-grain tablets, often referred to as antioxidant tablets.

For small quantities of wine, use 1 Campden tablet (7 grains) plus 1 antioxidant tablet per gallon. (Crush the tablets before adding them to the wine.) This combination, in terms of antioxidant effect, gives the equivalent of 3 Campden tablets per gallon. (Those Campden tablets would yield 180 p.p.m. of SO_2 in 1 U.S. gallon, 150 p.p.m. of SO_2 in 1 Canadian gallon – unacceptably high levels.)

For larger quantities, ½ ounce potassium metabisulphite plus ½ ounce sodium erythorbate in 120 U.S. or 100 Canadian gallons gives ample antioxidant action, yet still leaves only 18 p.p.m. SO_2 in your wine. That is much lower than most commercial wines contain at the time of consumption. Usual rates for commercial wines are 30 to 50 p.p.m.

I would emphasize again that these quantities are *not* adequate for sterilization in the preliminary stage of winemaking. The procedure described in this section is for use when racking or bottling wine, after fermentation is complete, and if you prefer to keep a low SO_2 level in your wine.

BARREL AGING

In *The Art of Making Wine* I pointed out some of the difficulties of barrel aging. I still would not recommend it to beginners; but the advanced winemaker, aspiring to produce premium-quality red or white wines, will undeniably get the finest results by using oak barrels.

An important development is that French oak barrels have recently become available to home winemakers. They are not cheap, and you won't find them in stock at every winemakers' supply store; but they *are* available and, if you are making European-style wines, the resultant extra quality can scarcely be overestimated.

I emphasize: get the French oak. It is a different species from the American oak that is sometimes offered in barrels. Moreover, the French oak is cut from the tree, then allowed to age for three years in the sun and rain, to bleach and leach various compounds and flavourings from the wood. Only after this thorough mellowing is the wood sawn into staves for barrel-making. The American cooper, by contrast, cuts his oak and runs it through a kiln to dry; that simply removes the moisture and leaves all the tannin and oils in the wood.

For barrel aging, you must be prepared to give a little attention to your wine at least every three weeks. You must sample it regularly because, even with the French barrels, you can get too much of the oak flavour. The oak should certainly not provide the single predominant flavour, but just enough to increase the complexity, and consequently the quality, of the wine.

After each sampling, the barrel should of course be topped up. Even if you don't draw off a sample, check the level repeatedly, because there is always a small loss when you are holding wine in oak.

As for size, the French vintners have found that the perfect size for a barrel is 66 U.S. gallons (55 Canadian gallons). That is too large for many home winemakers; you may find a good compromise in the 33 U.S. gallon size (27½ Canadian gallons).

Note that wine requires a *shorter* period of aging in the 33-gallon barrels than in the big ones. You will have to check it with particular care for excessive oak flavour. But, even in the 33-gallon barrel, you can usually age the wine for 6 to 12 months.

BOTTLING

Elsewhere I've mentioned various precautions you can take against the ever present risk of oxidation; but I suggest that the most important safeguard, once your wine is clear and stable – whether that takes 2 or 6 months – is to bottle it.

SIZE OF BOTTLES / The ideal container is the 26-ounce bottle. Once your wine is in these bottles, properly corked, there is very little risk of oxidation or contamination, and you can safely say you have wine that is aging. Moreover, it is aging faster in the 26-ounce bottle than in any bigger container. (I wouldn't recommend 13-ounce or 12½-ounce bottles; in these, because of the small volume, the wine will often age *too* quickly.)

I would issue a warning against the practice of storing wine in gallon jugs. That is not "bottling"! By my observation, more wine has been lost to oxidation or contamination in gallon jugs than in any other way. That's because the screw cap, which is the usual closure for these jugs, tends to loosen with temperature variations. Consequently your gallon of wine soon has little or no protection from air.

If you must use gallon jugs, at least take these two precautions: use new screw caps, and wrap a strip of half-inch masking tape around, so as to seal the cap to the neck of the jug.

ANTIOXIDANTS FOR BOTTLING / If you rinse bottles with metabisulphite solution before filling them, use a half-strength solution – 1 ounce metabisulphite crystals per gallon. Invert the bottles and let them drain briefly; but put in the wine before the solution loses all of its antioxidant value.

Immediately before bottling is also a good time to add a final light dose of antioxidant to the bulk wine. For each 5 gallons of wine, take 1 level teaspoon of antioxidant crystals, dissolve them in a little water, and stir into the wine; then proceed with the bottling. Then the metabisulphite and sodium erythorbate will come together in the bottle, and do the best possible job of preventing oxidation of your wine.

AIR SPACE / Never fill bottles or jugs right to the top. Always leave ¾ inch to 1 inch air space between the top of the wine and the cork, to give room for expansion of the liquid if the temperature increases during storage.

CODING / To eliminate the risk of forgetting which wine is in which bottle, it's a good idea to write a code name and date on the top of each cork immediately after bottling.

When the wine is mature, you can then label it before using it as a gift or serving it to guests.

STANDING OR LYING / Leave newly corked wine standing upright for 2 or 3 days; then, after the corks are set, lay the bottles on their side in a cool (57°F., 14°C.) place to age.

CLEANING

Standand techniques for cleanliness in winemaking were covered in *The Art of Making Wine*; but here is a special warning for advanced winemakers. The longer you keep on making wine in the same place, the more stringent must be your measures of contamination control.

What often happens is exactly the reverse: because he has not yet suffered any losses, the winemaker gets overconfident and begins to relax his precautions.

The most common error is leaving used vats, siphons or bottles to be cleaned tomorrow. "Tomorrow" perhaps turns into "next week", and then you find an epidemic of virulent spoilage organisms ravaging your winery.

Strong sulphite solution is a useful sterilant, but eventually some spoilage bacteria can develop a degree of immunity to it. You will do better to rely on heat, chlorine or TSP for cleaning your equipment; and, above all, make an invariable practice of cleaning it before you go to bed at night.

CLOSURES

There are now four types of closures readily available:

Screw caps – for social, still wines.

Crown caps – for 12-ounce bottles of pop wine.

Plastic stoppers – for champagnes or *vin ordinaire*.

Corks – for all table wines, fine sherries, ports and Madeiras.

BUYING CORKS / Corks have to provide protection for your best wines for a long time, so it's worth taking a little care in selecting and using them. Here are some pointers.

Avoid bargain-price corks; they are likely to be too old, or perhaps infected with parasites such as cork lice.

Good corks are usually sold by the gross and, at the time of writing, they are priced from $6 per gross upward. A good wine cork should be soft and fine-grained, about 45 mm. long by 23 mm. wide (1.14 ins. x .58 ins.).

Many American wineries use corks chamfered at one end or both ends. A chamfered cork, to be sure, is more easily inserted than the straight-sided cork. Yet, because of the chamfer, its length of contact with the bottle neck is shorter than that provided by the straight cork; therefore it offers a little less security than does the straight cork. It is significant that the French wineries have never adopted the chamfered cork.

Most American wineries use waxed corks. This might seem like a good idea to reduce the risk of leakage; but here again, note that the French wineries don't use them.

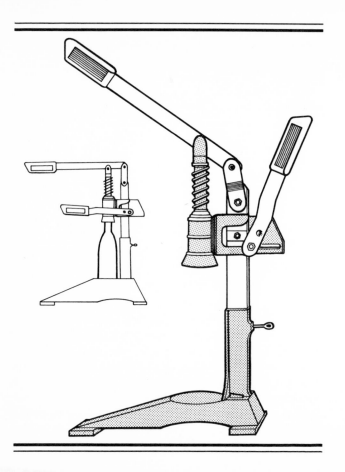

PREPARING CORKS FOR USE/Dissolve potassium metabisulphite, 1 ounce per gallon of water; soak the corks in this overnight, at room temperature. Use a plastic container, and make sure that all the corks are completely submerged.

If you have no time for the overnight treatment, soak the corks for 30 minutes in warm water without metabisulphite. (But remember that, if you use waxed corks, hot water could melt the wax off.)

Never boil your corks, especially in water containing metabisulphite. Boiling water and SO_2 disintegrate the cork.

CORKING MACHINES/There are now several kinds of corkers to choose from, but only two or three are worth considering.

This is not a book on how to save money. As an advanced home winemaker, you probably saved yourself several hundred dollars by making your own wine instead of buying it; but there are times when it's worth spending a little money. I don't approve of using gadgets for their own sake; but if there is a practical device that will save you time and labour, and improve the quality or appearance of your wine, then I say, "Use it!"

With corkers, the cheapest is definitely not the best. I would not, for instance, recommend the wooden corkers, even for one dollar apiece.

If you make 50 gallons a year or more, buy the French bench-model corker; it costs about $50, and makes bottling and corking effortless, a positive pleasure.

For less than 50 gallons a year, a French Sambri lever model at about $12 or a Danish plastic corker for under $5 will be adequate.

Remember when corking to lubricate the jaws of your corker—a light coating of vegetable oil every 6 to 8 corks.

CONCENTRATES

Most home winemakers are now familiar with grape concentrates, but since publication of *The Art of Making Wine*, the production of these has increased by leaps and bounds, their quality has improved, and many more varieties are available.

In the early and middle sixties, you simply could not buy top-grade wine grapes. But nowadays concentrates of such fancy varieties as Cabernet Sauvignon, Pinot Noir, Pedro Ximenez, Barbera, Zinfandel, Chenin Blanc, Riesling, etc., are being imported from France, Spain, Italy, Austria, Greece, Cyprus, Argentina and Australia; moreover, a complete range of varieties and qualities is being produced in North America, with the most modern equipment in the world, particularly in California.

It's impossible to say that any one country produces the best. The Spanish concentrates are certainly among the very best, but the Italian can equal them; and I have tasted wine from Austrian concentrates that was positively superb after aging in French oak barrels. As for the California concentrates, if properly used by the dedicated home winemaker (I shall explain later what I mean by "properly used"), they will give you better wines than you can buy from the average commercial winery in California. I know this sounds a bold statement, but I take into account that these concentrates are made by the latest methods available to food technologists and that, at home, you can process them without that close regard to the cost of ingredients that's necessary to any business operation.

COST OF CONCENTRATES / Some winemakers (mainly those who don't use them!) seem to think that concentrates are very expensive. Let's look at the facts.

First, consider the cost of fresh grapes. A good wine grape, such as Zinfandel, has recently been selling for $8.50 a lug (35 pounds); that's nearly 25 cents a pound. For fancier varieties, the price runs as high as 55 cents a pound.

You need around 16 to 20 pounds of grapes to make a gallon of wine, so you are paying 75 cents to $1.50 a bottle for wine made from fresh grapes. That's just the cost of the grapes; you have to do a good deal of work on them.

You cannot expect to produce top-quality wines

cheaper from grape concentrate than from the same variety of fresh grape. After all, someone else has done all the work of crushing and pressing, and has guaranteed the quality of the product. Using the concentrate, you save the cost of a crusher and press; you save a lot of time and labour. So, if you obtain good wine at 10 to 20 cents a bottle more than by using fresh grapes, you are getting a bargain.

Beware of cheap concentrates. In all probability, they will not be pure grape, but a mixture of grape, pear, sugar, syrup, water and acids – much like those "fruit drinks" you buy in the supermarket that look and taste something like fruit juice, but in fact don't contain the nutrients or quality of the real thing. Sure, these bargain-priced concentrates will yield a coloured alcoholic beverage; but there's some question as to whether it really deserves to be called wine.

SELECTING CONCENTRATES / Red concentrates must be really red, or blue-red – not orange or brown.

White grape concentrate should be very pale straw, or white, in colour. This quality is achieved only with first-rate equipment, controlled by top-notch food technologists, but it's the only kind suitable for good white table wines. Darker-coloured white concentrates should be used for sherries or dessert wines.

All concentrates should smell like fresh grape juice, certainly not like cooked or caramelized sugar.

USING CONCENTRATES / Remember that top-quality concentrates are not blended to achieve complete uniformity. Like fresh grapes, they vary from year to year; they even vary from one hillside to the next in the same vineyard!

This means that you cannot entirely rely on a recipe printed on the side of the container, or supplied by the distributor. Such a recipe is a useful guide – after all, the producers and distributors want you to be satisfied with the product – but there is no guarantee that it will apply exactly to the particular gallon of concentrate you are buying. You have to do your part, to get the best results.

After you have diluted the concentrate, check the sugar content. Even more important, check the total acids; these are certain to vary from one batch to another.

It would not be desirable for the manufacturer to try balancing the acid level by adding citric or tartaric acids, because the very process of concentration tends to take out total acids and increase sugar.

So it's up to you. You can make up for the shortcomings of the climate in the grape-growing region; you can overcome the defects of a bad year in a particular vineyard. You can adjust the sugar, adjust the acid, to optimum levels. The winemaker using fresh grapes has much more difficulty, and achieves less.

FALSE ECONOMY / I hear from some winemakers who

are disappointed with concentrates. In most cases, the disappointment comes from using recipes that excessively dilute the concentrate, making it into something far more watery than the original grape juice that came off the vine.

This was done in an attempt to produce wine economically, for 25 cents to 50 cents a bottle. I've already analyzed the real costs of wine from fresh grapes and concentrates. Grape prices are increasing year by year. You have to face this fact; you can't dodge it by adding extra water to your grape concentrate. If you just want *alcohol*, you can get it from sugar and yeast; but if you want *real wine*, you will be prepared to pay a little more to get it.

Part II of this book contains detailed recipes, but here are some guiding principles for getting the best results from grape concentrates.

WHITE RHINE STYLE WINES / Select either a Riesling concentrate or a very pale white concentrate; dilute with water to a specific gravity of 1.085 or a Balling of 21, and adjust total acids to .75. Add ¼ teaspoon of grape tannin per gallon. Use a German-type yeast culture and ferment in a cool place (60°-65°F.). When stable, fine or filter, and sweeten to 1% residual sugar before bottling.

WHITE BURGUNDY-STYLE WINE / Choose a white (pale in colour) Spanish, French or Italian concentrate. In this case, the source is not so important as the quality. As a general rule choose plastic-packed rather than canned concentrates for Burgundy (but there are exceptions). Dilute to S.G. 1.090 or 22 Balling and adjust total acids to .65. Add ¼ to ⅓ teaspoon of grape tannin per gallon. Use a Burgundy-type yeast culture and ferment at 65°-70°F. Age in French oak 2 to 3 months (or add oak chips); fine and bottle completely dry. Age 12 to 18 months in a cool place (57°F.).

RED TABLE WINE / Buy a deep red concentrate for Burgundy-type wine, and a light-coloured (but not orange or brown) concentrate for claret or Bordeaux type. Dilute to 1.090-1.095 or Balling 22-22.5 and adjust total acids to .65. Add ⅓ teaspoon of grape tannin per gallon. Ferment with Burgundy or Bordeaux-style yeast culture at 70°-75°F. Age in French oak if possible (or use oak chips) for 6 to 12 months. Fine with organic finings before bottling. Age 8 to 12 months in bottle.

DESSERT WINES / Sauternes are returning to popularity, and white grape concentrate lends itself well to producing sweet dessert wines. I like Spanish concentrates best for this purpose. Dilute to S.G. 1.120 or Balling 29; adjust acid content to .60; add ¼ teaspoon of grape tannin per gallon and ferment with a Sauterne yeast culture at 70°F. This should stabilize at a terminal gravity of 1.005. Age in French oak for 3 to 4 months. Fine or filter the wine;

sulphite it well (100 p.p.m.) and age in bottle for 2 years. This will be a luscious sweet wine, worth every cent of the $1.25 to $1.50 a bottle that it costs to make. (Above-average SO₂ is a characteristic of Sauterne, so it is an exception to the general rule of using only 50 p.p.m. SO₂ when bottling.)

FRESH GRAPES AND CONCENTRATES / You can pro-duce good wines from fresh grapes, and equally good wines from concentrates. Some winemakers think of these two methods as being mutually exclusive – you use either grapes or concentrate. Not so! The two methods may very well be combined; you can use fresh grapes *and* concentrates for the same batch.

The cost of wine from an expensive variety such as Cabernet Sauvignon can be reduced by using a concen-trate of some less expensive grape, without any detecta-ble loss of quality. Many commercial wineries blend different varieties of grapes; this is a perfectly respect-able and legal practice. In California, for example, it is permissible to apply a varietal label – say Pinot Noir – to a wine that contains only 51% of the named variety.

BLENDING / Let's look at this question of blended *versus* single-variety wines. There are two distinct approaches.

I think it is significant that most French wine is blended. The labels do not often mention the varieties of grapes that have been used, but rather the location of the vineyard, the year, and the name of the shipper or bottler.

Californians tend to emphasize the variety of grape; many of them seem to think that a wine made with 100% of one variety must be better than a blend.

Without a doubt, the *best* French wine is far superior to the best Californian. I have had hundreds of bottles of memorable French wines, but during the past ten years I've had only one bottle of California wine in the same class. That was a ten-year-old Napa Valley Zinfan-del, and it proved that California wineries *can* produce great wines. I think there are four reasons why they generally don't: neglect of careful blending, excessive filtering, disregarding vintage years, and insufficient aging.

(One hears the argument that California wine at $5 is a *better buy* than French at $25. That may be true, but it's not the question we're discussing now – that is, how to get *optimum quality*.)

So I'm wondering if the preoccupation with Cabernet Sauvignon and Pinot Noir grapes is justified, when the wines they produce in California are so different from those they produce in France.

I have made many gallons of 100% Cabernet Sauvig-non, but all my most interesting wines have been blends – either blended grapes and concentrate, or blended concentrates.

VARIETIES FOR BLENDING/It's important, in blending, to avoid combining varieties that conflict with each other; for example, Zinfandel does not blend well with Cabernet Sauvignon. You would do better to choose a blending grape or concentrate that does not have too strong a varietal taste or aroma, for example, Mission (red) or Tokay (white). Spanish concentrates made from Boval or Tintoreras (both red) blend well, and give colour and body without overwhelming the character of a fancy variety.

The Californian practice of using Thompson Seedless for blending can be risky. If you use very much of it, the Thompson flavour is detectable; it detracts from the quality of the varietal, and produces a wine that lacks vinousness.

The ideal blend is a combination of northern-grown French hybrid grapes with a suitable concentrate. This assumes a normal year, when the fresh grape is high in acid and the concentrate is low. But of course, not all years are normal. In a very warm year, the hybrids may have the right balance of acids; and in a cool, wet year, the concentrate will have enough acid, so that little or none need be added when you dilute it.

Your supplier should know the approximate acid level of the various concentrates he carries; but the safe way is to test and make sure.

BLENDING PROCEDURES/There are two ways to combine concentrate with fresh grapes: blending before fermentation, and blending fully fermented wines.

1/Blending before fermentation.

Mix the concentrate with water in the usual proportions. Crush the grapes and add the diluted concentrate to the pulp. Stir in thoroughly, and then measure specific gravity and acid in the usual way.

To calculate quantities, bear in mind that 1 gallon of concentrate is roughly equal to 100 pounds of fresh grapes. You know the weight of fresh grapes you are using, so you can easily determine the relative importance of the concentrate and the fresh fruit in the total batch.

2/Blending finished wines.

You can make wine from concentrate at any time of year, and hold it until you blend it with a batch of wine from fresh grapes. The purpose of blending is to produce a well-balanced wine and, sometimes, to reduce the average cost. Here are some hints.

a/Never blend an unsound wine with a good one. By "unsound" I mean one that is spoiled by bacteria or oxidation. Nothing will correct these faults; the bad wine will simply spoil the good wine you blend with it.

b/Wines should be at least 6 months old before blending; 8 months, or more, is better.

c/Test acid, alcohol and residual sugar levels of the

2. *A white wine and a red, before and after testing for acid.*

1. *"A corner for tasting . . . where wine-lovers enjoy fine wine."*

3. *A native North American,
the* LABRUSCA *vine.*

4. *The* VINIFERA *vine was imported
from Europe.*

wines before blending; this will give you a rough guide as to what proportions to use.

d/Bearing the analysis in mind, blend to suit your taste. Use a 1-ounce measure and mix 1:1, 2:1, 3:1 and so on until you reach a blend that suits your palate.

e/Remember that, in your wines, the acid and tannin should be rather too obvious; as the blended wines marry and mature, they will become softer.

f/Blended wines should have at least 3 months to marry—preferably longer—before bottling, and then should age 6 to 12 months in bottle.

COUNTRY WINES

In *The Art of Making Wine* I discussed the advantages of low fruit content in wines, and recommended that, except for grapes and apples, you use only 2 to 4 pounds of fruit per gallon. (Except for a few fruits of very low flavour-intensity.)

This procedure can be used with many kinds of wild and garden fruits. It yields a quick-maturing wine that does not have an overwhelming taste of the basic fruit, but compares well with a pure grape wine.

Yet some people feel that a wine with this low fruit content is rather thin for their taste. An easy remedy is to add some grape concentrate—red or white, whichever is appropriate. This will give you a full-bodied wine with more vinosity than the straight fruit wine.

Here is a basic formula for 1 gallon from which you can create your own recipes; or, if you wish, you can use it to modify some of the country wine recipes in this book.

For U.S. Measure	For Canadian (Imperial) Measure
2-4 lbs. fresh fruit	2-4 lbs. fresh fruit
13 fl. ozs. grape concentrate	16 fl. ozs. grape concentrate
Sugar to specific gravity 1.100	Sugar to specific gravity 1.100
1 gal. water	1 gal. water
¼ tsp. grape tannin where required	¼ tsp. grape tannin where required
½ tsp. pectic enzyme	½ tsp. pectic enzyme
Acid blend to 0.6%	Acid blend to .6%
2 Campden tablets	2 Campden tablets
1 tsp. yeast nutrient	1 tsp. yeast nutrient
Wine yeast	Wine yeast

The addition of grape concentrate will not appreciably change the acid content of the must; but of course, it contains a considerable amount of sugar. Make sure that the concentrate is completely dissolved, then measure the specific gravity of the must and add sugar to bring it up to 1.100. For a rough estimate of the amount of extra sugar required, use this formula:

1 lb. sugar added to 1 U.S. gallon will raise the S.G. approximately .044.

1 lb. sugar added to 1 Canadian (Imperial) gallon will raise the S.G. approximately .035.

FERMENTATION LOCKS

Basic instructions for the use of fermentation locks were given in *The Art of Making Wine*; but it's worth pointing out that a fairly common cause of failure is to leave the lock unattended too long, so that the liquid evaporates and the wine is left virtually unprotected.

Check fermentation locks every 2 to 3 weeks, clean them, and replace the metabisulphite solution. (When you are doing this routine task, you can also make sure that your secondary fermentors are topped up.)

FILTERING

Since *The Art of Making Wine* was published, there have appeared several filter processes suitable for home-made wines. So now, if a batch of wine does not clear naturally, or if finings are not effective as they usually are, you can use a filter; or if you are in a hurry to have star-bright wine, you'll find filtering much quicker than fining. Best of all, there is now a filter process that removes yeast from wine! This is the key to making finished wine in 10 to 15 days.

There are three main operating principles.

TYPE 1 Gravity is used to push the wine through the filter medium.

TYPE 2 Suction is used, with a device called an aspirator, that produces a partial vacuum and pulls the wine through the filter medium.

TYPE 3 This is a small-scale adaptation of the method used by commercial wineries: an air-pump creates pressure to force the wine through the filter.

Uses of Filters

For ordinary filtration – that is, for clearing a batch of cloudy wine – I believe that the gravity filters are best for amateurs: they are simpler, more foolproof, and much cheaper than the suction type.

TYPE 3 the pressure filter, gives 10 to 20 lbs per square inch pressure – much more than you can get with gravity feed; consequently it allows the use of a much finer filter medium, and is the only type that will actually remove yeast from your wine. (Yeast cells are so small that they pass through the other types of filter.) This pressure filter is what has opened the way to production of finished wine in 10 to 15 days from the start of fermentation.

None of the filters I have seen will process more than 10 gallons at a batch; then they require to be dismantled and have the filter medium cleaned or renewed. I still have not seen a practical filter for amateurs that will handle 50 to 100 gallon batches, and at present there are no indications of a breakthrough on that point.

Here I am going to review the five most readily available filter kits; but first I should mention two difficulties that may occur in filtering.

Trapped Carbon Dioxide

If you have CO_2 trapped in the wine, you will have severe difficulty in filtering; gas fills the siphon tube instead of wine, hence there is no pressure to push or pull wine through the filter. The remedy is to rack the wine before filtering it. The slight movement of the wine in racking will drive off any trapped CO_2.

Oxidation in Filtering

All filtering involves some exposure of the wine to air, and the slower the process, the greater is the risk of oxidation. Before any filtering, you would be wise to add anti-oxidant tablets or powder, Campden tablets or metabisulphite crystals. 1 tablet of each per gallon will be enough.

Grey Owl Filter

The Grey Owl filter I consider the best of the gravity filters; it works well and it is economical.

It is by far the easiest of all the filters to set up; there are only three component parts and it takes only two or

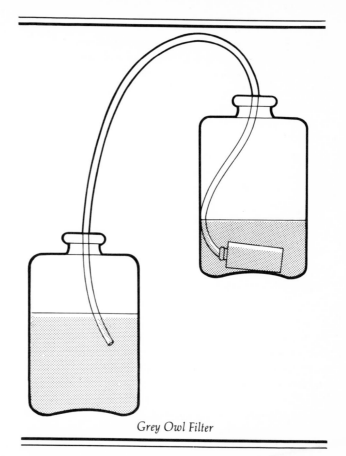

Grey Owl Filter

three minutes to assemble them. You do not have to fiddle with a variety of papers and powders: there are 6 dry cartridges, 3 standard, 2 fine and 1 very fine.

With a light haze, one run through will be sufficient; it takes 20 to 30 minutes to filter 5 gallons. With a heavy haze, you will need to use the standard filter first, then the very fine, or alternatively the fine filter first and then the very fine.

Our tests show that 10 gallons is the maximum you should attempt to filter through one cartridge; with a heavy haze, 5 gallons per cartridge would be plenty. Some people wash and re-use the cartridges; others feel it's best to use a fresh cartridge for each batch.

The original outfit, including 6 cartridges, sells for about $10; replacement cartridges cost about $1 each.

Harris Filter
This gravity filter has many components and takes a long time to assemble. It uses three filter media preparations, coat, cake and polish; the powders are easily spilled, and some people might find them difficult to measure. It does quite a good job of filtering, but is very slow indeed, and consequently there is more risk of oxidation than with the Grey Owl.

Initial cost: about $10. Filter media replacement package, $1.59. Compared with the cost of Grey Owl replacement cartridges, the Harris Filter would be slightly cheaper to operate.

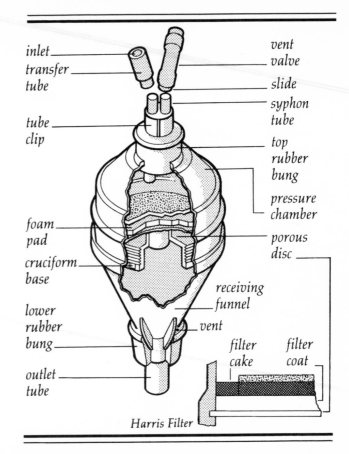

Harris Filter

Preliminary assembly of this gravity-type filter takes about 10 to 13 minutes; there are just a few parts, easily put together with nuts and screws. This work has to be done only once.

The filter medium is a single dry pad, easy to instal, easy to change and dispose of; it is good for only one use.

Each time you actually want to filter, there is another 5 minutes' work to get the apparatus ready; after use, it is easily cleaned in two parts.

You have to prewash the filter pad; this takes about 9 minutes' running time. The instructions suggest that you start the siphon running before balancing the liquid level and attaching the siphon to the filter. There is some seepage around the filter pad; this makes a little mess and wastes some wine – perhaps 3 to 4 ounces per gallon.

The Vinbright filter undoubtedly gives good results, but is exceedingly slow. On our tests, it took over 40 minutes to filter one gallon (not including the prewash time – just the filtering time after setting up). This slowness could give you severe oxidation problems.

For a single run, I think the Vinbright gives the best results of the three gravity filters – wine bright and clear after one filtering; yet I estimate that you could filter the same quantity of wine twice over with the Grey Owl filter and get as good or better results in less time.

Initial cost is around $14, and replacement pads

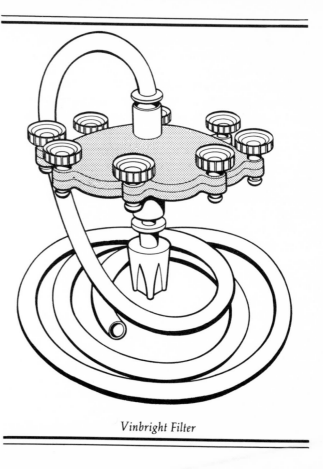

Vinbright Filter

around $1.15 each, so this is more expensive to operate than the other two.

Fessler Filter

This filter was designed by a highly respected professional enologist. It operates, not by gravity, but by the suction of an aspirator, a device that creates a partial vacuum, powered by the flow of water from a tap.

The apparatus is quite complicated, and takes about 20 minutes to set up, including a process called "precoating" the filter screen. It requires a careful adjustment of water pressure, to be sure that water does not get into your wine.

The rate of filtering is rather slow, about 5 gallons an hour. The apparatus costs $60 to $70, and replacement filter medium is about $5 a package—by far the most expensive of the systems we have tested.

Vinamat Filter

The Vinamat pressure filter, when properly used, filters a gallon of wine in 5 to 7 minutes, and delivers it sterile—yeast-free—directly into your bottle or jug. It can be refilled and ready to go again in a couple of minutes; and it will filter 2½ gallons of wine before you need to change the filter pad. Here are some notes on its construction and operation.

The wine that is to be filtered is put in the *pressure tank*, which is made of heavy, strong plastic, with a maximum

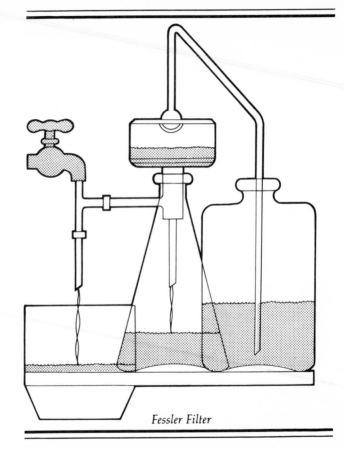

Fessler Filter

capacity of 5.5 litres (approximately 1.5 gallons).

The *air pump* is screwed on to the top of the pressure tank.

The *input tube* carries the wine from the pressure tank to the *center ring* of the filter.

From the center ring, the wine is forced outwards, through the two *filter pads*, into the concentric circular grooves of the *top* and *bottom pressure plates*.

It then goes through the two *outlet tubes* to the *Y-piece*, thence through the *bottling tube* to the bottle or jug in which it is to be stored.

1 / Unscrew the nuts that fasten the three sections of the filter together.

2 / Take two clean filter pads (they are thin white disks) and fit one into each of the top and bottom pressure plates. The two sides of the filter pad are not alike; one side is flat, with many small indentations, and it has some printing on it – the trade name, and a word to indicate one of the three textures: coarse, fine or sterile.

(*N.B.* "Sterile" means the ultra-fine texture, that removes all micro-organisms such as yeast cells, and leaves the wine sterile.) *Important: the side with the printing on it must be touching the circular grooves of the pressure plate! If the pads are inserted the wrong way round, the filter will not work properly.*

3 / Reassemble the filter. It fits together like a clubhouse

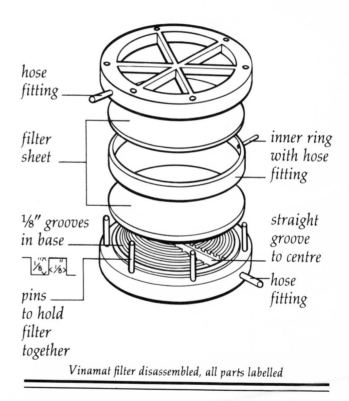

hose fitting

filter sheet

1/8″ grooves in base

pins to hold filter together

inner ring with hose fitting

straight groove to centre

hose fitting

Vinamat filter disassembled, all parts labelled

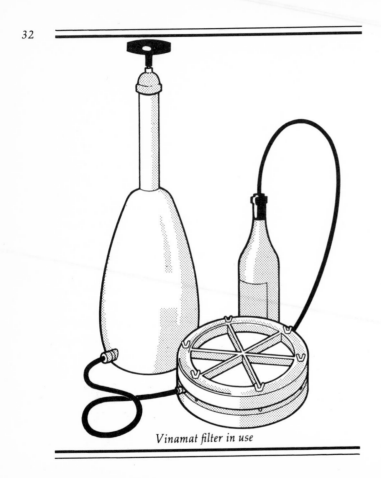

Vinamat filter in use

sandwich: bottom pressure plate, filter pad, center ring, filter pad, top pressure plate. Screw down all the wing nuts, till they lightly touch the top pressure plate; then tighten them *two at a time, by opposite pairs. i.e.* suppose the nuts were numbered clockwise, you first tighten nos. 1 & 4, then nos. 2 & 5, then nos. 3 & 6. There's no need to use great force: just tighten until you can feel the components are firmly held together.

4/Before you use it for wine, the filter should always be primed with water to ensure the most efficient action of the filter pads. Dissolve 1 teaspoon of acid blend in 2 litres (about half a gallon) of water, put it in the pressure tank and screw on the air pump. After several strokes of the pump, you will see water flowing through the outlet tubes and Y-piece, and out of the bottling tube. You can let it run down the sink. Finally, to get the pressure tank empty, tilt it so that the last of the water runs into the input tube.

5/This priming process has caused the filter pads to swell slightly, so tighten the wing nuts a little more.

6/Now you can begin to filter your wine. Unscrew the pump and put a batch of wine into the pressure tank. *Important: never completely fill the pressure tank!* The maximum safe level is clearly marked on the side of the tank. Screw on the pump, and pump until the wine starts flowing. Note: there is still some water in the filter itself, and the tubes; so for a little while, although wine is going through the input tube, water is still coming out of the bottling tube. Watch this closely, and as soon as wine begins to come out, put the tube into the first bottle. (When filtering white wine, you may have to taste what is coming from the filter to know when it's wine and not water. Simply dip your finger in the flow from the outlet tube.)

There's no need to pump hard, trying for excessive pressure; just pump steadily, enough to keep the wine flowing smoothly.

To stop filtration at any time – say to get more bottles, or to answer the phone – simply unscrew the pump enough to release the pressure, and the flow is instantly stopped.

7 / After the first batch has been filtered, unscrew the pump, put in more wine, and resume operations. One pair of pads will, on the average, filter about 10 litres, or 2½ gallons of wine. By the time you've nearly reached that limit, the filter pads are beginning to get clogged, and you may find that the filter begins to leak a little. So some winemakers stand the filter in a shallow dish or pan, to avoid any mess.

8 / The filter pads are not reusable. Even if you only filter one gallon, you can't save the pads for use at a later date. So, for economy, it's best to filter 2½ gallons at a time.

After you have finished, dismantle the filter and throw the pads away. Wash all parts thoroughly with soap and water, or detergent, and pump some water through the tubes.

Our experience shows that, once you are familiar with the operation of the Vinamat, you can filter and bottle 2½ gallons of wine in 30 minutes, including setting up, and cleaning up afterwards. As for efficiency, we have tested wine filtered by this process by keeping it at 70°F. (21°C.) for two months, without any sign of renewed fermentation: this proves that all yeast was removed!

The Vinamat can be used for all kinds of wine filtering operations, with coarse, fine or sterile pads, whichever is appropriate. But many readers will be specially interested in its use to make finished wine within 10 to 15 days from starting fermentation. This process is described in Part II, Section 7.

At the time of writing, the Vinamat sells for about $45.00 and filter pads are about 50 cents each. If you don't expect to use the filter often, many winemakers' supply stores will be renting the filters by the day, complete with one set of pads in place, ready for priming. Finish your 2½ gallons, then you just return the filter to the store, with the used pads still in it. What could be simpler?

Here are a few pointers on the buying and growing of wine grapes.

Let me begin by saying that one cannot be dogmatic about the qualities of this or that individual variety among the 5,000 or more known varieties of *vinifera* grapes—not to mention the numerous North American grapes, and all the hybrids.

There is a great deal of confusion about the naming of grape varieties grown in Europe and North America, South Africa and Australia. In some cases, the same grape is called by different names in different places; some varieties developed in North America have been misnamed; and the origin of some varieties has been forgotten.

Often, too, a grape variety that is successful and popular in one country has mutated, or has yielded inferior wines, when transferred to another.

Even from grapes that are unmistakably of the same variety, you may get wines ranging from excellent to mediocre or poor, because of differences in soil, climate and viticulture.

The same vines, in the same vineyard, tended with the same measure of care and skill, produce much better grapes some years than others, simply because the weather varies from year to year.

With all these reservations, then, I will mention some varieties that have won wide acceptance among experienced winemakers.

RED GRAPES / Here are some of the best-known red grapes grown in California, Oregon and some parts of the State of Washington:

Cabernet Sauvignon	Pinot Noir
Zinfandel	California Gamay
Barbera	Petite Sirah
Sangiovetto	Ruby Cabernet
Grenache	Carignane
Mission	Alicante Bouschet

Cabernet Sauvignon and Pinot Noir are by far the most popular and famous of the California red grapes. Yet I think that, with careful processing, you can do just as well with some of the varieties from northern California, such as Zinfandel, Barbera, Petite Sirah or California Gamay.

Some people are very happy with Ruby Cabernet, a *vinifera* hybrid which has a very subtle spiciness.

Carignane and Mission are generally grown in the warmer parts of California; they do not have a great character of their own, but are often used as blending grapes. (Mission is cheap for a *vinifera*.)

Alicante Bouschet has a very deep red juice, but such a strong aroma that, to my taste, it is somewhat overpowering, and unsuitable for varietal wines; it is principally used as a blending grape for the sake of its colour.

Grenache is very popular for making rosé; but, when grown in California, its juice often has a definite yellow or orange tinge. I think it has altered noticeably from its European forebears.

WHITE GRAPES

Johannisberger Riesling	Emerald Riesling
Gray Riesling	Chardonnay
Gewurtztraminer	Semillon
Sauvignon Blanc	Chenin Blanc
Sylvaner	Palomino
French Columbard	Green Hungarian

Chardonnay, a very fine grape, is sometimes called Pinot Chardonnay or Pinot Blanc. At its best, it yields a prestigious white wine comparable to French white Burgundy. But it is very expensive; it does not ship well; and, unless it is grown in cooler areas, it does not yield the kind of wine that one would expect for the price.

Semillon is a beautiful grape; its wine, if properly made, with a slight residual sweetness – say 1% – is excellent.

Chenin Blanc is used in France to produce the Vouvray wine. The California-grown Chenin Blanc yields a wine that, while unmistakably different from Vouvray, yet is very fine in its own right. This wine, too, needs a slight residual sweetness.

As for Green Hungarian, I can't discover what is the origin of this grape, or what is its name in Europe. It does not have a good reputation, yet I have tasted some excellent white wine made from it in California. It's definitely worth trying.

The Palomino is the most easily available white grape outside of California; many fruit-produce firms handle it. Palomino has a rather indifferent flavour; it is best used as a blend with other white grapes, or in wines like Sherries and Madeiras. Yet I would not want to be too severe on Palomino; it can be surprisingly good if grown far enough north.

Gewurtztraminer is quite popular, yet it has a very fragrant or flowery aroma, which definitely requires some getting used to. You might call Gewurtztraminer wines an acquired taste.

HYBRID GRAPES

A hybrid is a cross between two different varieties of grapes. The ideal result is to produce a strain that has the desirable qualities of both its parents, and none of their defects. On this continent, the major objective has been to produce hybrids that have the typical resistance to disease and to climatic extremes of the North American varieties, while yet retaining the fine flavour and the winemaking qualities of the European varieties.

This interbreeding has been going on for many, many years. Thousands of strains have been developed, but not many have been successful wine grapes. The few good wine varieties, however, have won acceptance, not only in North America, but also in parts of Europe.

Philip Wagner has laid out 8 grape-growing areas with varying climatic conditions, and lists the types of native or hybrid grapes best suited to each area. I live in Area No. 8, for which Wagner recommends the following grapes:

Seibel White, 5279, 9110, 13047
Seibel Red, 10878, 9549, 5279, 13053
Red, Baco No. 1, Foche.

I have had excellent red wine from Seibel 9549, grown in District No. 5. In fact, it is the only good red wine from a hybrid that I've tasted. Foche and Seibel 10878 make tolerable red wine in some years, but the *riparia* (one of the native North American grapes) comes through quite strongly in the Foche wine.

The listing and recommending of hybrid grapes is becoming difficult because wineries are creating names to replace the original numbers of the more desirable varieties. No doubt a name will look better than a

"I'll never understand how that cactus has grown so big!"

number on the label of a varietal wine, but the changeover is going to leave a long trail of confusion for authors and winemakers. If you want to keep up to date on these changes of nomenclature, the best source of information is the American Wine Society. Their members include some of the most knowledgeable vine growers in America outside the State of California, both amateur and professional.

GROWING YOUR OWN GRAPES / Important: There is a great difference between growing grapes for your own wine (where you don't have to make a profit) and growing grapes for a living. So anyone who is thinking of starting a commercial vineyard should not attempt to apply the principles discussed here. Instead, consult your government department of agriculture; it can usually supply you with the history of, and the prospects for, grape culture within its jurisdiction. Local offices of the agriculture department may be able to give more detailed advice about local soils and climatic conditions. Universities and agricultural colleges may also be helpful.

Now let's get on with the subject of growing grapes strictly for your own use.

VINIFERAS OR HYBRIDS? / Here's the first point on which the hobbyist wine-grower has an advantage over the commercial vineyard. In many areas the experts will say, "You can't grow *viniferas* here!"

But often, what they really mean is, "You can't grow *viniferas* here *on a commercial scale.*" They mean that *viniferas* will not give a profitable crop every year, and in some years may fail altogether.

I would point out that the *viniferas* are hardier than is commonly supposed. Eastern Canadian wineries did produce a true Pinot Chardonnay varietal wine that was very successful on the market—so successful, indeed, that the demand apparently persuaded the producer to blend with hybrids or North American varieties.

New York State, Washington and Oregon and, in Canada, the Niagara Peninsula and southern British Columbia, are largely planted to hybrids or North American varieties for commercial winemaking. Yet in all these regions, *viniferas* such as Riesling or Pinot Chardonnay—even Pinot Noir and Sauvignon—will grow, if carefully tended in a protected area, where it would not be feasible to grow them commercially.

Maybe two years out of five, you might not get a crop from these vines; but when you do, and the grapes do ripen, they will yield you a wine vastly superior to any you could make from hybrid grapes. Remember, you are not working for high yield, but for *high quality*.

And don't overlook the possibility of growing them in a greenhouse, if you have space to build one.

But if, after careful research, you decide that it's quite

impossible to grow true *viniferas*, then you should consider the French hybrids.

HOME WINERY AND STORAGE CELLAR

If you are making wine in fairly large quantities – say 50 gallons or more a year – a proper arrangement of your space can make the work easier and the wine better. If you can possibly manage it, the best way is to have three separate sections, for these three purposes:

1 / Primary fermentation
2 / Secondary fermentation and bulk storage
3 / Storage of bottled wines.

1. Primary Fermentation Area

a / STRUCTURE. Area, about 10 feet by 12.

Easy access to the outside, so that equipment (some of it, like barrels, fairly bulky), grapes, and other fruit and ingredients can easily be brought in, and used pomace easily disposed of.

A floor that can be washed down and sterilized with chlorine or other sterilants.

A heating system and insulation adequate to maintain a steady temperature of 70°-75°F. (21°-24°C.) for primary fermentation. (This, of course, is far too warm for storing finished wine.)

Low humidity. This is desirable at all stages of wine processing and storage; dampness encourages the growth of spoilage organisms.

A good-sized laundry tub or sink (two tubs or sinks would be better) with hot and cold taps threaded to take hose connections, bottle-washer, etc.

b / LIGHTING. Adequate artificial lighting is important, but fluorescent lighting is *not* good; it has much the same effect on food products as sunshine, and tends to hasten deterioration. Ordinary incandescent lighting is better.

c / EQUIPMENT. A ventilation fan, to exhaust the large quantities of carbon dioxide formed during primary fermentation, and also to reduce the concentration of sulphur dioxide in the air when you are sterilizing equipment.

Strong benches to keep your primary fermentors about 2 feet off the floor.

A large workbench where you can do various types of analysis; it will also hold your corker, capper and other bottling equipment.

Racks where you can stack washed bottles for draining.

Shelves for storage of equipment and materials – hydrometers, ebulliometer or alcohol refractometer, corks, caps, chemicals, various additives, etc. All this should be visible and properly labelled.

An electric pump and hoses for filling and emptying large fermentors.

2. Secondary Fermentation

a / STRUCTURE. Area, about 80 square feet, with easy access to the primary fermentation area, so that you can run hoses or pumps back and forth for easy cleaning of barrels or carboys.

A floor that can be washed down and sterilized, because there will be wine spilling from barrels, carboys and gallon jugs.

Temperature control, the same as in Area 1.

b / LIGHTING. Same as in Area 1.

c / EQUIPMENT. Strong benches to hold barrels and carboys well off the ground, so that you can easily move wine by siphoning or pumping. Also, for barrels, this allows you to put in spigots and run wine into bottles, and then take them to Area 1 for corking and labelling.

(*N.B.* If it's not possible to separate these two areas, they can be combined into one space of 150 to 200 square feet.)

3. Storage Area

Here your precious end product – the bottled wine – is aging, and becoming all the time more valuable. So it's worth taking the trouble to obtain optimum conditions.

a / STRUCTURE. An ideal location is the northeast corner of a basement – the coolest spot in the house, with a minimum of vibration and light.

Anyway, this storage area should definitely be removed from the production area, which is too warm, and too frequently lighted, for good storage conditions.

As for size, allow space for *at least* a thousand bottles - preferably much more. You will probably be storing not only the wine you make yourself, but also some commercial wines you have bought, that are being kept for further aging or for special occasions.

Very important! You must be able to lock this area securely, to exclude casual intruders, neighbours, relatives or children. You need a strong door, with high-quality dead-bolt lock or padlock; window openings strongly barred or completely blocked up. Bear in mind that, when full, this cellar contains thousands of dollars' worth of wine. Guard it as carefully as you would the same quantity of cash.

Ideal temperature for this area is 55°-60°F. (12°-15°C.) Slight gradual temperature variations will do no harm (*e.g.*, a few degrees warmer in summer than in winter); but rapid temperature changes (*e.g.* up and down every 24 hours) will seriously impair the condition of your wine. It is well worth the trouble of putting extra insulation around this area, to keep the temperature as nearly constant as possible.

b / LIGHTING. Complete darkness is desirable, except when you are actually using the area; and no fluorescent lights!

c/EQUIPMENT. Bottles sealed with screw caps, crown caps or plastic stoppers should be stored upright; for these, ordinary wooden shelves will serve very well. Strong bookshelves, or boards laid across concrete blocks, are good. You can also get strong adjustable steel shelving, with slotted uprights that let you vary the shelf-spacing to suit the size of bottles you are using—30-oz. pop bottles, 26-oz. wine bottles, gallon jugs, or beer bottles.

Corked bottles must be kept lying on their sides, so that the corks don't dry out. This raises the problem that a bottle lying flat is likely, at the slightest jog, to start rolling; and that's bad for the wine it contains. So you need some sort of fixture that will support the bottles and hold them still.

To convert ordinary shelving into bottle racks, you can lay the corrugated bottoms of egg cartons upside down on the shelves; these will hold your wine bottles still.

Specially shaped wooden bottle racks are good; useful racks can also be improvised from cardboard wine boxes laid on their sides, or empty fruit juice or grape concentrate cans stacked up in tiers. (Of course, you need some firm support at the ends to stop the tiers collapsing.)

A particularly good rack is made from clay drain tiles laid on their sides. These have two major advantages: they hold the bottles steady, with a minimum of vibration, and they tend to keep the temperature of the wine stable.

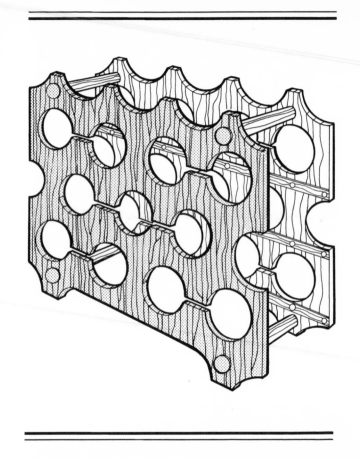

I have even seen strong wire netting, with three-inch to four-inch openings, used for extra-large wine racks.

d / OPERATION. Even within a cool wine cellar, there will be some differences of temperature; so each type of wine should be placed in the zone that best suits it. Put your dessert wines and liqueurs on the upper racks, where the air is warmer; below these go the red table wines, and below them the white table wines; right at the bottom, in the coolest air, go your sparkling wines.

Some of the wines in your cellar will be in bottle for periods of ten years or more; and no wine will ever age properly if you have to keep pulling bottles off the racks to see what's in them.

There's no need to stick a full label on every bottle of wine you produce; but you must have some kind of identifying code number or mark on the cork, or on the glass, where it can be read without moving the bottles.

You also need a record book in which, for each batch, goes a listing of the type of wine, with details and dates of its production, number of bottles, and a note of where they lie in the storage area.

The book also includes a tally of bottles consumed, so that you know at any time just how much of each batch is left.

Notes on the quality of the wine at various dates will serve as a guide to the aging of future batches.

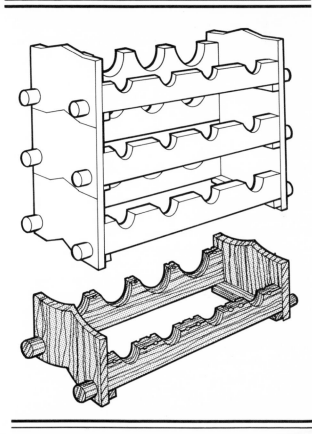

To facilitate finding the wine you want, small cards pinned or stuck to the racks will show exactly what's where.

e / TASTING. If you have space in this third area, set aside a corner for tasting; a table, some old-fashioned wooden benches, some tasting-glasses, candlelight – it can be a place where wine-lovers enjoy fine wines in an atmosphere reminiscent of the ancient cellars in the wine-raising countries of the Old World.

ALL AREAS / Important! Under no circumstances, in any of the three areas, should anyone be permitted to smoke! Wine, in primary fermentors, in carboys, or even in bottles, will readily absorb unwanted odours or flavours; and very few indeed are the wines in which an admixture of cigarette, pipe or cigar smoke is not a change for the worse.

A true connoisseur, no matter how he may enjoy his tobacco elsewhere, will know better than to smoke in this hallowed environment.

JUDGING WINE

Wine is made to be enjoyed. Yet many people will say, "This is a nice wine," or "I liked that wine better than this," without being able to say exactly *why* one wine pleases them, or exactly *how* one wine is better than another.

"Delightfully full and round!"

I certainly wouldn't urge anyone to learn the esoteric verbiage of the wine snob, the man who can't really enjoy his wine because he is so busy criticizing it. Yet I do suggest that it's worth while developing some definite standards by which to judge wine.

By those standards you can assess your own skill as a winemaker; you can increase that skill by accurately judging the merits and shortcomings (if any) of each batch of wine, and so learning what you should do to make the next batch even better.

Using the judging system described here, you can accurately compare your wines with those of other home winemakers, or with commercially produced wines.

And, equally important, if you know exactly *why* you enjoy a wine, you'll undoubtedly find that you enjoy it *more*, because it now gives you an intellectual as well as a sensual pleasure.

THE 20-POINT SCORING SYSTEM / This judging technique depends on sampling a wine, giving it points for its good qualities, and witholding points for defects. A wine rating 17 to 20 is outstanding of its type, with no marked defect. (I might say there are very few wines that reach this level of excellence.) A score of 13 to 16 indicates a good wine with no character defect; this is where most of your home-made wines will fall. Nine to 12 shows a low-standard wine; 5 to 8 shows some serious defect, definitely not acceptable. Wines scoring less than 5 points are completely spoiled, and would not be considered drinkable.

Some winemakers and drinkers used to use a 100-point system for judging wine; but it was found that most people did not use the entire scale, and restricted their scoring to 20 points or less. So this 20-point score sheet was developed by the University of California at Davis, the foremost school of enology in North America.

This scoring system forces a logical evaluation of wines; it encourages the use of descriptive words that are meaningful to everyone – acid, yeasty, bitter, flat, sweet, and so on. It does not require a large vocabulary of esoteric terms.

With this system, and about 6 hours' practice, the average person can become capable of judging whether a wine is good or bad and, if it's bad, deciding exactly what's wrong with it. This is particularly useful for the winemaker; once you know what's wrong with a wine, you have a chance to correct it, or in any case you can prevent the same fault from occurring again.

A SAMPLE SCORE / Let's see how the system works on a sample of red table wine. (*page 54*)

You can make your own score sheets on a duplicator; or many winemakers' supply stores sell them.

Name	Date		Type	

Quality	Possible Points	General Comments	Points Given
Appearance or Clarity	2	*Star bright*	2
Colour	2	*Deep red, blue tinge, young*	2
Aroma and Bouquet	5	*Full fruit aroma, not vinous yet*	4
Total Acid	2	*Slightly high; may mellow in time*	1
Sugar	1	*Completely dry*	1
Body	2	*Adequate, but red wine needs more*	1
Flavour and Balance	3	*Good for young wine; time may help*	2
Astningency (Tannin)	1	*Adequate*	1
General Qualities	2	*More promising than rewarding*	1
Total possible points	20	*Total points awarded*	15

Now let's look at the various terms on the sheet, and see how to score for each of them.

APPEARANCE OR CLARITY/maximum: 2 points. Examine the wine both in the bottle and after it has been poured into a glass. A perfectly clear wine scores 2 points: "brilliant" and "star bright" are expressions sometimes used. A small, *firm* sediment at the bottom of the bottle is not objectionable; but if the sediment is loose or if, on decanting, the wine becomes slightly opalescent, the score is only 1 point. If the wine is noticeably cloudy, or contains visible suspended particles suggesting contamination, it scores zero. (Hold the filled wineglass up to the light to check for suspended particles.)

COLOUR/maximum: 2 points. Colour, of course, must be judged according to the type of wine, and there is room for some variance within each type. For example, a white wine can vary from white with a tinge of green to green-gold, and rate 2 points; if it is deep golden, or light brown, it earns 1 point; if dark brown or reddish, zero.

For red wines, the colour should be appropriate to the grape or other fruit that was used. An unduly thin, watery appearance in wine that should be dark, or an unwanted brownish tinge in a wine that should be red, for example, might reduce the score to 1 or zero, depending on how far it departed from the ideal.

AROMA AND BOUQUET / This is the most important category, with a maximum score of 5 points.

Aroma is the smell of the ingredients; bouquet is the smell that develops in a properly made wine during aging. Therefore, if you are judging a new wine, you will not fault it for lack of bouquet, if you think it has potential.

To bring out the aroma and bouquet, it's a good idea to swirl the wine around inside a glass; this exposes more of its surface to the air; then sniff at the mouth of the glass.

Now suppose you are judging a mature wine made from Muscat grapes; here are some hints on scoring.

A distinct aroma of the grape: 3 points. If it also has a good vinous bouquet: 5 points.

No identifiable aroma or bouquet, but no unpleasant smell: 2 points.

A slightly unpleasant smell – say, just a hint of sulphur dioxide, or a rubbery odour: 1 point.

A vinegary or spoiled smell, definitely unpleasant: zero.

TOTAL ACID / *maximum*: 2 points. The section on "Acid Content" indicates, for various types of wines, acid levels that yield optimum results for the average palate. Score accordingly.

Acid content correct for the type of wine: 2 points.

A slight excess or deficiency of acid, perceptible to the taste: 1 point.

A substantial excess or deficiency, noticeably unpleasant to the taste: zero.

SUGAR / *maximum*: 1 point. In this category, there's no grading to be done: either the sugar content is correct for the type of wine, or it is not.

For example, a red table wine, to score 1 point, should be completely dry. If it has any detectable sweetness, it scores zero.

In a white table wine not specifically designated "dry", 1% to 2% residual sugar is acceptable and scores 1; excess sweetness would score zero.

In a Cream Sherry, you expect 8% to 12% residual sugar, and a definite sweetness; here lack of sugar would score zero.

BODY / *maximum*: 2 points. Body is particularly important in red table wines; it is a feeling of fullness on the palate that has nothing to do with sweetness. (Lack of body is a weakness – among others – that follows from excessive dilution of concentrates.)

In white table wines, body is less important; they can be slightly sweet and rather thin.

Full-bodied (appropriately for the type of wine): 2 points.

Medium, but adequate: 1 point.

Weak-bodied, excessively thin wines: zero.

FLAVOUR AND BALANCE / maximum: 3 points. The flavour of a wine is made up of many different elements; all should be pleasant, and none of them should unduly dominate the others.

A pleasing flavour, appropriate to the type and age of the wine, will score the full 3 points here.

Deduct points for bitter, yeasty, metallic, caramelized, alcoholic (hot, dry), or any other unpleasant flavours.

Note: do not confuse this with the "General Qualities" item that follows. Here, under "Flavour and Balance", you are not asked to say how you personally like or dislike the wine, but to judge whether its flavour and balance are good and appropriate for its type. You do not have to like Vermouth, for example, to be able to recognize a good one.

ASTRINGENCY (TANNIN) / maximum: 1 point. The correct quantity of tannin makes an important contribution to the character of a wine. Too much tannin makes a wine harsh or rough-tasting; too little leaves it flabby and insipid. It is not, at first, the easiest element to detect; tannin may be confused with acidity, or masked by a high content of alcohol or residual sugar. Nevertheless, the training method described below will enable you to assess it accurately.

Tannin should be more pronounced in red wines than in white. Young wines often exhibit excess tannin, but this is not necessarily a fault, as it may, with aging, drop to the optimum level.

GENERAL QUALITIES / maximum: 2 points. Under this heading you express your personal reaction to the wine.

If it scores well on other items, if you like it, and you wish you had it or knew where to buy it, score 2.

If it is a sound wine – *i.e.*, has no serious technical defects – yet you don't particularly like it, score 1.

If the wine has some definite defect, and you would not want to drink it or serve it, score zero.

THE STUDY GROUP / The easiest way to develop wine-judging ability is in a group – 10 is a convenient number – under the guidance of someone who already has a fair knowledge of the subject. This is the ideal approach for a winemaking club or a gourmet society. So I will first describe an effective way to run such a group, with an instructor. Later I will offer some suggestions for two or three people working without an instructor.

Prepare for 7 sessions, each of 1 to 1½ hours. The interval between sessions should not be longer than a week, or students tend to forget what they have learned; two sessions a week is the best schedule. As for time, the earlier in the day the better: the students' palates will be fresher. If it must be in the evening, ask the students to refrain from drinking any alcoholic beverage earlier in the day, and to eat a bland supper. There should be no smoking immediately before, or during, the tasting sessions.

There should preferably be 5 wineglasses for each student, or at least 2 glasses each, with facilities for quickly washing used glasses. (Note: if glasses are being washed during sessions, don't pour wine into them while they are hot from a dishwasher or from rinsing at the sink. Make some arrangements to cool them to room temperature before they are used again.)

Everyone should have access to a spittoon or pail, to spit out the wine after tasting. Some of the samples will have defects such as excess acid or tannin, and no one wants to swallow that – it would impair the palate for further tasting. There should be a supply of cold water and crackers to refresh the students' palates after each taste.

It would be convenient to have two stewards to pour the wine, wash glasses if necessary, and serve the water and crackers.

Also each student will need, for each session, 5 copies of the score sheet.

THE BASIC PROCEDURE / The best way of learning to judge the good and bad qualities of wine is *by comparison* with a known standard. In the section on "Acid Testing" I suggested the use of a norm, a vial of untreated wine, by comparison with which you can detect subtle colour changes in the vial on which you are making the acid-test. Similarly, in the first three wine-judging sessions, students will compare a norm – a glass of good-quality wine – with samples of the same wine that have artificially created defects.

This, for beginners, is much easier than comparing two or more different wines; it also has the advantage that the defects can be made fairly severe – more so than in most commercial wines – and therefore easier to detect.

SESSION 1: RED TABLE WINE / The instructor should buy, in advance, some good dry red wine. You should know the wine you select; it must be good or fine, and properly mature. Score it in advance; it must merit at least 14 out of 20 points, because this is going to be your norm, your standard of excellence, and if it is *not* excellent, the whole session will be a fiasco.

If you can, get 6 half-bottles, 12½ or 13 ounces each. If you can't get the half-bottles, buy 3 26-ounce bottles and rebottle them in half-bottles.

For this first session, concentrate on detecting four faults: excesses of acid, tannin, sugar and alcohol. To one 13-ounce bottle add 1 teaspoon of citric acid; to the second, add ½ teaspoon of grape tannin; to the third, add 3 teaspoons of granulated sugar; and to the fourth add 1 ounce of grape brandy. In each case, first dissolve the additive in a little of the wine, to get an even distribution, and mark each bottle as you doctor it, so that you know which is which. That leaves 2 half-bottles, or 1 26-ounce bottle, of sound wine.

The preparation should be done on the day of the tasting session, so that the wine with the added sugar will not have time to start fermenting. Also test the acid content of the oroginal wine (it should be close to .65%) and similarly test the high-acid sample.

For the tasting session, the wine should be at room temperature – at least 65°F. Now you are ready to begin.
1 / Serve everyone an ounce of the norm, and show them how to assess the first two items on the score sheet, Appearance or Clarity, and Colour. Mark score sheets.
2 / Swirl the wine in the glass and sniff its Aroma and Bouquet; the wine should score at least 2 or 3 points here. Mark score sheets.
3 / Now for the taste. Make sure the students know they are not to swallow the wine. Fill the mouth with the full ounce of wine; "suzzle" it, *i.e.*, take in air at the same time if possible; hold it in the mouth for a few seconds, making sure that it comes in contact with all parts of the tongue; spit nearly all of it out, allowing just 2 or 3 drops to go down the throat.

Now run down the other items on the score sheet, explaining how many points you are giving, and why. It's as well, at this first session, to assume that none of the students has any expertise; thus none of them will be made to feel inadequate.

Everyone now has a completed score sheet, all with the same score, as a reference.
4 / The students should now rinse their mouths with water and, if desired, nibble a cracker. (Repeat this after each sample has been tested.)
5 / Now repeat the whole process with the first faulty sample – the one with excess acid. Use a clean score sheet. Don't leave them to guess about the defect: this is not an examination. Mention the original acid count, and the increased acid count, and get students particularly to try and note the increased acid taste produced by this specific percentage increase of acid.
6 / Repeat with the high-tannin sample, similarly explaining the fault.
7 / Repeat with the high-sugar sample.
8 / Repeat with the high-alcohol sample.
9 / To conclude, repeat the whole testing procedure with the remainder of the norm.

SESSION 2: WHITE TABLE WINE / Buy 3 bottles or 6 half-bottles of German or California white wine. Get them a week in advance, because the first fault to be demonstrated this time is oxidized wine. To prepare this sample, open one half-bottle and leave it open at room temperature for 7 days.

The other 3 faults are to be vinegar contamination, excess sulphur dioxide, and low alcohol. These 3 samples can be prepared on the day of the session. To one half-bottle, add 1 teaspoon of household vinegar; to the next, add 2 crushed and dissolved Campden tablets; to the last, add 3 to 4 ounces of water.

This white wine would normally be served chilled; but for testing we want to accentuate taste and smell, so cool it only to 50°F.

Proceed as before: first let everyone test the norm, which should score 14 or more out of 20. Mention that in this wine 1% to 2% of residual sugar is acceptable; let the students note the degree of sweetness produced by this sugar percentage.

Repeat the test with the four defective samples, and conclude with a final test of the norm.

SESSION 3: STILL ROSÉ WINES / Buy two bottles of good California still rosé and one of good New York State still rosé. Both wines should be as dry as you can get. You can check them for degrees of residual sugar with a testing kit similar to those used in diabetes for urinalysis; for winemakers the kit is marketed under the trade name Dextro-Chek.

The important thing is that both wines have similar degrees of residual sweetness, because for these training sessions the students should not be presented with too many variables at once.

As usual, the wine should be in half-bottles for treatment. One of the California rosé samples must be prepared 5 days in advance, to demonstrate low acid. Add 1 teaspoon of calcium carbonate or precipitated chalk. Watch for foaming, and put it aside to settle.

Then, on the day of the tasting sessions, proceed as follows:

Sample No. 1 (the one described above): carefully rack the wine off the deposit into a clean half-bottle.

Sample No. 2, California: add 1 teaspoon citric acid.

Sample No. 3, New York State: a few hours before serving, add 3 teaspoons of dissolved sugar.

This session will demonstrate the bitterness of low-acid wine and the difference between the labrusca and vinifera flavours, and will also prove the function of residual sugar in creating balance and enhancing flavour in the labrusca wine. (Many people find that they enjoy a dry vinifera wine, but not a dry labrusca.)

SESSION 4: APERITIFS, SWEET AND DRY / For this session, get three Sherries: a Spanish Amontillado, a medium Canadian and a medium American. There is no need for the artificial creation of faults in this session; the aim is to judge the differences between the three wines as they come from the bottle.

Begin and end with the Amontillado. Note that, by comparison, the Canadian Shenry is thin and lacks aroma. The U.S. Sherry has body, but has· a burnt flavour, like Madeira, since it is produced by a Madeira-type cooking process, not by a solera process under Flor Sherry yeast.

SESSION 5: CHAMPAGNE / Buy three different Champagnes: one European, bottle-fermented, and two American, one of which should be bulk-fermented, and the other artificially carbonated. (The method of processing should be on the label of each.)

SESSION 6: DESSERT WINE / For this session, get 3 bottles of port: one Portuguese, one Californian, one Canadian. For additional variety, you can also add a bottle of white port.

SESSION 7: REVIEW / Prepare samples of dry red table wine, much as you did for the first session, but preferably with a different wine.

This time, don't say anything about the defects of the samples as they are served: let each student mark his score sheet without any help from you. At the end, simply read your own score sheet for each numbered sample; let the students compare theirs, but not necessarily reveal how well any of them has done.

Most of them will be delighted with their success; they should be encouraged to practise using the technique at home.

HINTS FOR SMALL GROUPS / For one, two or three people working without an instructor, it's obviously wasteful to spoil whole bottles or half-bottles of wine by creating artificial faults. So get some small glass vials, holding about one ounce for each person who is going to take part; prepare your samples in these, number them so you know which is which, and proceed to taste them in the order described above.

One practical point, for individuals or small groups: don't hurry from one sample to the next. Allow ample time for your nose or palate to refresh itself after one test before you begin the next.

MEASUREMENTS

Teaspoon and cup measures of solid ingredients such as acid blend, yeast nutrient, sugar, etc. always refer to *level* teaspoons, *level* cups, etc.

PLASTIC CONTAINERS

Collapsible plastic secondary fermentors (Cubitainers) are frequently offered to beginners, either in winemaking kits or separately. True, they are economical; but many of them are unsatisfactory as secondary fermentors, because they "breathe"—that is, they permit passage of air. If you keep wine in one of these containers at 60° to 70°F. for more than a couple of months, you will get excessive oxidation.

There are some secondary fermentors now being produced of very high-density plastic. They are usually marked "Food Grade" and cost as much as glass, if not more; but they are satisfactory for the purpose. So, before you buy a plastic secondary fermentor, inquire and make sure that it is made of the high-density, food-grade plastic.

As a further check, carefully smell the inside of the container. Some manufacturers do not maintain a very high level of quality control; their plastic products have a residual odour, which will certainly be picked up by the first wine that is placed in them.

SERVING WINE

There are many books on serving wine; even some cookbooks include a section on it. I think that many of these writers are too rigid with their rules on how to select wines for various purposes, and they lay too much stress on the formalities of serving it. Some people, understandably irritated by this system of taboos, reject all the rules.

I suggest that between these two extremes there is a happy mean — a sensible approach to the use of wine.

WINES WITH FOOD / Originally, the accepted table wines were dry white or dry red, and these were just about the only wines many people ever tasted.

Visiting friends at three in the afternoon, the neophyte may be handed a big glass of absolutely dry, full-bodied rough red wine. Of course, without any food, it tastes terrible.

The victim timidly says, "I'm afraid I don't like this; it tastes a little bit sour to me."

The host says, "Oh, but red wine *must* be dry!"

The guest is made to feel like a social misfit. He never realizes that the wine that tastes so harsh alone would be an enjoyable accompaniment to a beefsteak or roast; the dryness of the wine would then not seem excessive, because of the salt on the food.

Or again, some people, in the middle of the evening, will bring out a bottle of dry white Burgundy or Alsace Riesling; even if the wine is really cold, it is still too dry to be enjoyable after dessert and coffee, without some appropriate food to accompany it.

So there's really no argument about the proposition that table wines must be served with food; but nowadays the term "table wine" embraces considerably more than those good old, reliable dry reds and whites!

For example, suppose you serve a slightly sweet fruit salad, or shrimp with a sweet sauce, at the start of a meal; for such dishes, a sweet white wine is appropriate and delicious — for example, one of the white German wines with 1% to 3% residual sweetness.

Or those same wines, well chilled, can be served as an

aperitif before you start on the food, and because of their low alcohol content you can drink a fair volume without impairing your palate.

There's not much dispute that delicate fish and chicken simply won't tolerate a rough red wine; or that with lamb or beef a white wine tends to be overwhelmed. Nevertheless, many people do not like red wine at all, and consequently will use and enjoy white wines with all forms of food.

SHERRY / A medium-dry to dry Sherry is an excellent aperitif; but the medium-dry and sweet Sherries can be taken at any time, either with cookies and cheese, or by themselves. Sherry is now often being served on the rocks, so that it will be thoroughly chilled. Such a procedure may horrify the wine formalist; yet it is going to continue, because many people are now drinking more wine and less distilled spirits.

MIXED AND DILUTED WINES / The old rules on wine use are more relaxed in Europe. Mixing Champagne, or other white wines, with Cassis or black-currant liqueur, is quite common, and tastes delicious. In Greece, they serve a medium-dry Ouzo or Anise, diluted with water; it makes an excellent aperitif. Dubonnet or Campari with ice and soda are also very popular.

I think the term "social wine" originated with the home winemakers; but now the commercial winemakers are using it. Social wines are sweet, with a moderate alcohol content – say 13% to 15% by volume – and taste nice to most palates. They can be made from grapes, berries, apples, peaches, or a whole range of other fruits; the residual sugar tends to bring out the fruit flavour, and make the wines pleasant to drink without food on social occasions.

These social wines are now frequently being served mixed. They are very pleasant with soda, or any mixer that's not too strongly flavoured; they are delicious over ice, with the addition of sliced oranges, maraschino cherries, etc.

CHAMPAGNE / I think that amateurs should make more Champagne; the commercial Champagnes are among the most expensive of wines – in many places they bear a heavy tax burden. So, if they are well made, they are particularly suitable as a gift for a friend (if local law permits it).

I like to drink Champagne liberally, on an appropriate occasion. A slightly sweet Champagne can be delicious either before or after dinner; almost everyone will enjoy it if it is well made and well chilled.

ROSÉ WINES / You will find rosé wines very widely acceptable as a social drink, or as an accompaniment to most foods (though to my taste rosé comes off rather poorly with red meat).

If you're planning a party, and have doubts about whether some of your guests are wine drinkers, you can't go far wrong in serving sparkling rosé with just a hint of sweetness; almost everyone enjoys this, and for newcomers to wine drinking, it's an excellent introduction. (Many of the pop wines, I think, were inspired by sparkling rosé.)

My own preference is for a rosé with a hint of sweetness, but in rosés there's a wide range—from dry to sweet, in still and sparkling types. Really, there's a rosé for every taste and every occasion.

WINE GLASSES / Now for a few thoughts on the glasses from which the wine is to be drunk. The use of properly chosen wine glasses is not just a bit of snobbery. The serving of wines with decorum and respect heightens the pleasure you obtain from them.

For a start, the wine should be poured from an elegantly prepared bottle, suitable to the wine, or from a nice decanter.

Good, all-purpose wine glasses (see illustration) can be used for many different wines. But a fine white wine, I think, does come across better in the tall Rhine-style glasses.

I strongly oppose the use of the flute-type Sherry glasses; they hold too small an amount of wine, and they are very susceptible to spilling, usually in the process of serving. Spanish-type Sherry glasses, now coming more

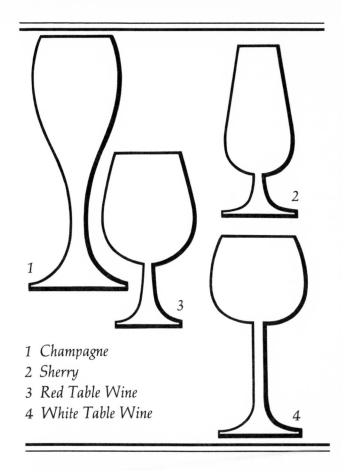

1 *Champagne*
2 *Sherry*
3 *Red Table Wine*
4 *White Table Wine*

widely into use, are much better: they don't spill, they hold somewhat more and, most important of all, they let you enjoy the delightful nose and aroma of the Sherry.

Another one I don't like is the small, saucer-shaped Champagne glass. To be sure, it makes the Champagne go further, but that's its only advantage. A tulip-shaped glass conserves the aroma and the bubbles and, in my opinion, gives you a much more satisfying drink of Champagne.

SPARKLING WINES: TWO MORE METHODS

Several techniques for making sparkling wines were described in *The Art of Making Wine*. Here are two more.

SODA SIPHON METHOD / With this process, you can take 32 fluid ounces of any still wine, and turn it into sparkling wine, or pseudo-Champagne, in a few minutes.
1 / Get a standard soda siphon – the rechargeable type that uses metal bulbs or "bombs" of compressed carbon dioxide; it has a capacity of about 32 fluid ounces.

Unscrew the top and nemove the stem – the long tube that goes to the bottom of the container. Make sure you put back the rubber gasket.
2 / Take the wine you want to use; get it very cold – as cold as you can without freezing it – and put it in the siphon.
3 / Screw down the top, put in a fresh carbon dioxide

bulb, and shake the siphon vigorously to get the CO_2 dissolved in the wine.
4 / Very carefully, over the sink, press the trigger and let the excess CO_2 escape. (The wine will not come pouring out, because you have removed that siphon stem inside.)
5 / When you have released the excess CO_2, unscrew the top of the siphon and pour the wine into glasses. You'll find that it is now sparkling.

Note: This method does only one siphon-full at a time; but as long as you have a supply of wine ready-chilled, you can repeat the process quite fast, and so get a nearly continuous supply of sparkling wine.

Prepared like this, the wine will not sparkle quite like Champagne; the bubbles won't hang in there, but tend to dissipate fairly quickly. To get a really long-lasting sparkle, prepare the siphon-full of wine and leave it overnight; then the CO_2 will be more fully dissolved in the wine, and the sparkle will continue long after you pour it, as it does with Champagne.

DEEP-FREEZE METHOD / A number of Calgary Wine-Art customers have pioneered a modification of the Andovin Champagne method described on pages 158-9 of *The Art of Making Wine*.

Let's summarize that method first, then describe the new twist that makes it easier.
1 / To the basic dry wine, add 2 ounces per U.S. gallon

(3 ounces per Canadian or imperial gallon) of dextrose in syrup form, ¼ teaspoon per gallon of yeast energizer, and Andovin all-purpose wine yeast (1 package per 5 gallons).

2 / Bottle in 30-ounce soft-drink bottles and seal with crown caps.

3 / When fermentation is complete, put the soft-drink bottle and a clean Champagne bottle into the freezer and chill to about 26°F. (-4°C.)

Remove both bottles. Carefully siphon the wine from the soft-drink bottle into the Champagne bottle, leaving the sediment behind. Presto! Champagne without sediment!

Unfortunately, many people find that the siphoning procedure causes a lot of problems and frustrations. So here's an alternative technique.

Follow the same procedure for steps 1 and 2 as described above. Then:

3 / When fermentation is complete, set your freezer at 0°F. (-18°C.) and once it reaches that temperature, put the soft-drink bottles of wine in the freezer for 1¼ hours.

4 / Put into the freezer a clean Champagne bottle for each soft-drink bottle already there. Leave for another 15 minutes.

5 / Take out one soft-drink and one Champagne bottle at a time (holding them with oven mitts or a towel). Uncap the soft-drink bottle and pour the wine directly into the Champagne bottle, leaving the sediment behind.

The wine, at this temperature, will retain the carbon dioxide in solution. Insert a Champagne cork and wire it down.

(For a sweet wine, add ½ to 1 ounce of wine conditioner to each Champagne bottle before putting it in the freezer.)

Congratulations and thanks to those winemakers who developed this simple, effective method!

STERILANT SOLUTIONS

You will often need a sterilant solution for filling fermentation locks, and for sterilizing equipment. To make a small batch, dissolve 3 Campden tablets in 4 fluid ounces of water.

Note: Some copies of *The Art of Making Wine* contain a misprint on p. 24: 1 tablet to 4 ounces water. The mixture of 3 tablets to 4 ounces given here is the right proportion.

For larger quantities, dissolve 2 ounces potassium metabisulphite crystals in one gallon of water; keep it in a tightly stoppered bottle.

This solution contains about 7500 parts per million SO_2 – enough to make unwanted micro-organisms turn in their chips fast! It should, of course, never be added to wine at any stage of processing.

Note that this solution, in use, gives off sulphur dioxide, which can be unpleasant or even unhealthy, if you inhale too much of it. For example, suppose you are scrubbing a 20-gallon primary fermentor with the solution; don't stick your head down inside it and breathe deeply!

As a general precaution, when using strong sterilant solutions, work in a well-ventilated place and avoid excessive inhalation of SO_2.

SUGAR

Some winemakers have asked me about the various sugars and sugar substitutes that are on the market; so here is a list of the different types and their uses in winemaking.

SUCROSE/Pure sucrose is ordinary refined white granulated sugar. It makes no difference whether it comes from the sugar cane or the sugar beet; the two products are chemically identical.

This is the most easily available form of sugar, and the cheapest. It imparts no flavour to the wine, and is readily hydrolized (converted from a disaccharide to a monosaccharide) by the acid in a normal must, therefore easily converted by wine yeasts into carbon dioxide and alcohol.

(Readers of *The Art of Making Beer* will have noticed that I do not recommend cane or beet sugar for beer-brewing; that's because the beer ingredients do *not* contain enough acid for quick, effective hydrolization of sucrose.)

DEXTROSE/Corn sugar is pure dextrose, a monosaccharide. It is chemically quite suitable for winemaking, and does not alter the flavour of the wine. But it is not so easy to obtain as sucrose; it costs more per pound and, moreover, you have to use 20% more of it than sucrose to get the same alcohol content in the finished wine.

DARK SUGARS/There are a number of dark-coloured sugar products such as ordinary brown sugar, Demerara sugar, and various forms of molasses and sweet syrups. They are brown, either because they have not been completely refined, or because caramelized substances from the sugar-making process have been added to them.

These dark sugar products are more expensive, and harder to obtain, than the pure sucrose, and they would certainly spoil the flavour of table wine, or any wine where you wanted a delicate fruit flavour.

They are used, in moderate quantities, for some strong-flavoured, dark-coloured, high-alcohol wines such as tawny port, Madeira, or Old Brown Sherry. There the Madeira-like flavour of the dark sugar is welcome; but for other wines it is unacceptable.

OTHER SUGARS/You may sometimes see white sugars sold at fairly high prices under such names as berry sugar, candy sugar, etc. These are all pure sucrose, and

5. Right / This cloudy red wine needs fining..
   Left / The same wine after fining.

6. Racking from primary fermentor to secondary fermentor.

7. Left to right: Burgundy, Claret, Chablis, Sherry, Rosé.

have no advantages for winemaking over pure cane or beet sugar.

SUGAR AND ALCOHOL YIELDS

There is considerable controversy among amateur winemakers regarding the relationship between hydrometer readings of the must and the potential alcohol content of the finished wine. It's a typical example of the age-old conflict between theory and practice, between the man who pins his faith on mathematical projections, and the other man who just likes to go ahead and see what happens. Unfortunately, for this problem, neither approach is absolutely correct.

It *is* important to make a fairly accurate estimate of the strength of your wine. If you overestimate its alcohol content, then the wine is less stable, and more subject to contamination, than you thought.

So let's see what are some of the problems, and how far we can resolve them.

THE HYDROMETER / There are difficulties in marketing an accurate hydrometer.
1 / It must be mass-produced to keep the price down.
2 / If the same instrument is to serve for wines, ciders and beers, it must have a broad range.
3 / For general use, it must be sturdy, even though this reduces accuracy.

So, for good results, it's wise to get the best hydrometer you can afford, and treat it very carefully.

THE MUST / Suppose you have a must of S.G. 1.090 (22° Balling). Some people, calculating potential alcohol yield, reason thus: "S.G. of pure water = 1.000. The difference, .090, is fermentable sugar, and the French Dujardin scale says that this much sugar will yield 12.6% alcohol by volume."

But Dujardin, or any other similar scale, can give only an *approximate* figure for potential alcohol; that's because there are several variables, any of which can markedly alter the final result:

1 / Unfermentable solids.
The S.G. reading of 1.090 is measuring, not only sugar, but also an assortment of unfermentable substances such as acids, tannin, pectin, fruit pulp and colouring matter. These things are important for the flavour and appearance of the wine; they register on the hydrometer as soluble solids; *but they don't produce alcohol.*

A must of low fruit content, or one made from carefully filtered concentrates, will tend to have less of these unfermentable solids than would fresh grape juice, say, or fresh apple juice. So a low-fruit-content must of S.G. 1.090 might produce 13.3% alcohol by volume, instead of the expected 12.6%.

2 / Yeast.

Different strains of yeast show different degrees of efficiency. Take two batches of identical must, and ferment them with different yeasts; one might yield 1% to 1.5% more alcohol than the other.

3 / Fermenting conditions.

The functioning of the yeast – and hence the production of alcohol – depends on the operating conditions – temperature, oxygen supply, etc. Only if all conditions are perfect will the maximum alcohol conversion be attained.

BE CONSERVATIVE / So, with the limited facilities and the contamination hazards faced by most amateurs, I would opt for a conversion table that errs on the conservative side.

For example, Dujardin says a must of S.G. 1.090 will give 12.6% alcohol, whereas the table at p.171 of *The Art of Making Wine* says 12%.

The dedicated or scientifically minded winemaker will eventually learn which musts have less unfermentable solids, and so can use a lower starting S.G. But in the meantime, he will not have had any wines spoiled because of unexpectedly low alcoholic content.

SUGAR AND SPECIFIC GRAVITY

For sweetening wine at intermediate stages of fermentation, you can use white granulated sugar. The effect is measured by checking the increase of specific gravity produced.

The same quantities of sugar will produce the same sweetening effect on a finished wine, but then wine stabilizer must be added as well, to prevent a renewed fermentation.

Quantities

4 ozs. sugar added to 1 U.S. gal. raises S.G. .012.
4 ozs. sugar added to 1 Canadian gal. raises S.G. .010.
Or, to express it another way, to produce an increase in S.G. of .010, you should add:
For 5 U.S. gals., 16½ ozs. sugar
For 5 Canadian gals., 20 ozs. sugar
(*c.f.* item on Wine Conditioner).

SULPHUR DIOXIDE CONTROL

You are aware of the need for adequate, but not excessive, levels of sulphur dioxide at various steps of the winemaking process. Some degree of control is attainable by using known amounts of metabisulphite; yet many winemakers will be glad to have a more exact method.

You can also use it to test the SO_2 level of commercial wines from various sources, for comparison with your own finished wines.

A simplified test procedure for free sulphur dioxide was developed by Fred Eckhardt, and is described here by his permission.

A complete test kit is available, containing the following items:

Equipment

A 20-cc. graduated plastic syringe

An eye-dropper

A test flask of about 100-cc. capacity (3.5 fl. ozs.).

Ingredients

Iodine solution of a strength described as N/40. (Store this in a refrigerator when not in use.)

25% sulphuric acid, H_2SO_4

1% starch solution.

The iodine solution, sulphuric acid and starch solution can also be bought separately at winemakers' supply stores.

CALIBRATING THE IODINE SOLUTION / The iodine solution, even when kept refrigerated, is slightly unstable, so it must be calibrated afresh each time you use it.

a / Prepare a test solution of known sulphur dioxide content by completely dissolving 1 Campden tablet in 1 gallon of water. Then you have:

In 1 U.S. gallon, 65 parts per million free SO_2.

In 1 Canadian (imperial) gallon, 50 p.p.m. SO_2.

b / With the plastic syringe, measure 50 cc. of the test solution into the flask. Rinse the syringe.

c / Add 10 cc. sulphuric acid. Rinse the syringe again. *Important precaution*: Always add the acid to the test solution (or to water, wine or other liquid). *Never* add water, solution or wine to the acid; that could cause a violent reaction, throwing the acid up into your face.

d / Add 5 drops of starch solution with the eye-dropper. Rinse the eye-dropper.

e / Now draw 10 cc. iodine into the syringe. Add 2 cc. of it to the flask, then continue adding it drop by drop until the test solution turns blue. If the iodine is fresh and full strength, it will require about 4 cc. to make the colour change in the U.S. test solution (65 p.p.m.) and 3 cc. in the Canadian test solution (50 p.p.m.). If the iodine is weak, it will take more than that to produce the colour change. Anyway, note exactly how much iodine you have used; you should be able to read it to half a cc.

f / The strength of the iodine is expressed by a figure we call the Iodine Factor. Calculate it from this formula:

$$F = \frac{S}{I}$$

where F = Iodine Factor, S = SO_2 content of test solution (65 for U.S., 50 for Canadian), I = number of cc. iodine used.

For example, suppose that with the U.S. test solution you used 4.5 cc. iodine. Therefore $F = \frac{65}{4.5} = 14.4$.

Or with the Canadian test solution, you used 3.5 cc. iodine. Therefore $F = \frac{50}{3.5} = 14.3$.

Now you are going to test your wine sample with this same iodine solution; so the Iodine Factor tells you that, for every 1 cc. of iodine you use, the wine contains 14.4 (or 14.3) parts per million sulphur dioxide.

TESTING THE WINE/Now repeat the process with wine instead of with the test solution.

a/Measure 50 cc. of wine into the test flask.

b/Add 10 cc. sulphuric acid.

c/Add 5 drops starch solution.

d/Add the iodine very carefully, right from the start, as little as ¼ cc. at a time, if you can. When the colour change occurs, note exactly how much iodine you have used.

e/Multiply the number of cc. iodine by the Iodine Factor, and the result is the SO_2 content of the wine in parts per million.

For example, suppose $F = 14.4$.

Amount of iodine used = 1.5 cc.

Then 14.4 x 1.5 = 21.6.

There are 21.6 p.p.m. SO_2 in your wine.

It's advisable to try the test a few times on white wine to get used to it. The colour change is more difficult to see in a red wine; it will not show a clear blue, but will turn noticeably darker, to a brown or blackish hue.

CORRECTING DEFICIENCIES/What if you discover that the SO_2 level is too low? For example, suppose you had completed the test described above on a batch of wine after the first racking in the secondary fermentor. A suitable SO_2 level at this stage would be 30 to 50 p.p.m.; but this wine has only 21.6 p.p.m. (call it 22 for simplicity). So you want to put in another 8 p.p.m. or thereabouts.

Use Campden tablets, bearing in mind the above-mentioned formula:

1 Campden tablet in 1 U.S. gal. gives 65 p.p.m. SO_2.

1 Campden tablet in 1 Canadian (imperial) gal. gives 50 p.p.m. SO_2.

A simple calculation will show the effect of Campden tablets on bigger quantities.

U.S. gallons:

1 tablet in 2 gals. gives 32.5 p.p.m.

1 tablet in 5 gals. gives 13 p.p.m.

1 tablet in 10 gals. gives 6.5 p.p.m., and so on.

Canadian gallons:

1 tablet in 2 gals. gives 25 p.p.m.

1 tablet in 5 gals. gives 10 p.p.m.

1 tablet in 10 gals. gives 5 p.p.m., and so on.

Now suppose it's a 5-gallon batch of wine you are working with. You add 1 Campden tablet. That brings the SO_2 content up:

$22 + 13 = 35$ p.p.m. (U.S.)

$22 + 10 = 32$ p.p.m. (Canadian)

If you want to achieve finer degrees of control, or if you are working with smaller batches, you can even use a half or a quarter of a Campden tablet.

CORRECTING EXCESSES / If you find the SO_2 level is too high, you can remove free SO_2 by pouring the wine back and forth from one container to another, or by stirring vigorously.

SWEET WINES BY PASTEURIZATION

Many winemakers who are no longer intimidated by the dry-wine snobs want to produce a stable wine of moderate alcohol content containing some residual sugar. In sweet, still wines of the white Rhine or Moselle type, for example, with 9% to 11% alcohol, the 1% to 2% residual sugar enhances the flavour of the grape or other fruit, and makes an excellent dessert wine.

You can, of course, sweeten such wines with wine conditioner, or with sugar syrup and wine stabilizer; but there is a third method – pasteurization – where controlled heat is used to kill the wine yeast.

Pasteurization is usually thought of as a means of preserving milk and foodstuffs; most beer-drinkers do not realize that commercial breweries pasteurize canned and bottled beer to prevent renewed fermentation during storage. You can just as well do it with wine.

1 / Make your wine in the normal way, using the hydrometer to ensure that you end up with no more than 10% to 12% alcohol by volume.

2 / When the wine is clear and stable (probably 3 to 6 months after the primary fermentation), make some sugar syrup, 2 parts sugar to 1 part water, and use this for sweetening the wine. The degree of sweetening must be determined by your own taste (experiment with a small measured sample); but for most people 2 to 3 fluid ounces of this syrup per gallon will be enough. Stir it in thoroughly.

3 / For the usual small, pre-bottling antioxidant treatment, add 1 Campden tablet per gallon, or rinse the bottles with standard metabisulphite solution.

4 / Bottle the wine, taking care that its level is 1 to 1¼ inches below the bottom of the cork or screw cap. *Adequate air space here is important.* Leave one bottle open.

5 / Immediately put the bottles in a canner or large pot that will hold 6 to 12 at a time. Pour water into the pot till the water level is about 2 inches below the tops of the bottles; this means that most of the wine is immersed in the water. Put the pot on the stove and turn on the heat.

6 / To check the temperature of the wine, put into that uncorked bottle a thermometer with a range up to 220°F. (104°C.) Use a floating thermometer if you have one; if not, tie a string on the thermometer so that it won't drop right into the bottle. Anyway, the thermometer must be well immersed in the wine.

7 / Keep applying heat until the temperature of the wine in the open bottle reaches 165°F. (74°C.). This means that the wine in the closed bottles is also at the same temperature. All the yeast cells have now been killed.

8 / Take the pot off the stove, put it in the sink, and start running cold water into it. Promptly cork or cap the open bottle. Keep the water running until the wine is cooled to room temperature. It is now stable and clear, and there will be no renewed fermentation.

9 / Age the wine as usual. The heat of pasteurization will have driven off all the sulphur dioxide from the bottle that was open; so that one may not be quite as good as the rest.

Note: Some wines are not "heat stable"; that is, heating to 165°F. may turn them cloudy, or make them throw a precipitate. Commercial wineries often heat their wines to see if they are heat stable; if not, they would of course filter a cloudy wine, or rack one that threw a precipitate. However, the problem should not occur often enough to prevent you from using this process.

SPARKLING WINES / Many people – myself included – like a slight sweetness in sparkling wines and ciders; a similar procedure can be used to produce them.

1 / Begin with a clear, stable wine of not more than 12% alcohol content, and sweeten it with sugar syrup (2 parts sugar to 1 part water). Depending on the degree of sweetness you want in the finished wine, add from 4 to 6 fluid ounces of syrup per gallon, but no stabilizer or other additives. (Tasting at this stage will *not* indicate the final taste of the wine, since some of the sugar is going to be used up to produce the sparkle.)

2 / Put the wine in Champagne bottles, closed with wired stoppers, or in soft-drink bottles sealed with crown caps. As with the still wines, leave an inch, or a little more, of air space between the wine and the closure. *Important*: The bottles must be absolutely sound, to withstand the high pressure built up during pasteurization.

3 / Put the bottles in a warm place (about 75°F., 24°C.) for 48 hours.

4 / After 48 hours, inspect the bottles; there should be a noticeable sediment of yeast, proving that active fermentation has begun. Cool one bottle to about 55°F. (13°C.), then open it to determine that there is enough sparkle in the wine.

Forty-eight hours is usually enough for cider; but with wines over 10% alcohol it may require 72 hours, or a little longer, to develop enough sparkle.

But don't wait too long! Remember, the heating will almost double the pressure of gas in the bottle; so if you wait to achieve too much sparkle, you run a definite risk of bottle explosions.

5 / Pasteurize as with the still wine; but watch the temperature closely, and take great care not to let the wine go above 165°F. (74°C.) In all probability, if the temperature of the wine reaches 155°F. (68°C.) that will be enough to kill the yeast.

You now have a clear, sweet, sparkling wine that will remain stable without any additives.

TABLETS

Any ingredient in tablet form—Campden tablets, wine stabilizer tablets, etc.—must be crushed before use, to ensure complete solution as quickly as possible.

TROPICAL FRUITS

Good white wines can be made from tropical fruits such as papaya, chirimaya, mango and passion fruit; prickly pear (cactus) yields a beautiful rosé. If you live in a warm climate, you may have some or all of these fruits available; but, for dependable results, you will have to take certain precautions.

A problem is that, in tropical regions, fruit naturally carries only a small amount of good wine yeast, but a very large number of spoilage organisms. There is also the pectin in the fruit to be dealt with.

So, for all such fruit, use the preliminary process described below; it is much the same as "blanching" in the cookbook sense of the term.

Place all the fruit you are going to use in a boilproof plastic vessel and pour on enough vigorously boiling water to cover it completely. Let it steep for 5 minutes; then pour off the water. The skin of the fruit is now sterilized, ready for you to begin the normal winemaking procedures.

WINE CONDITIONER

To sweeten a finished wine, you can add sugar syrup to suit your taste; then, to prevent renewed fermentation, you will have to add a wine stabilizer as well (unless you use the previously described pasteurization method).

A convenient alternative is to use wine conditioner, which sweetens and stabilizes the wine simultaneously.

Wine conditioner consists of two ingredients. The sweetening agent is a clear syrup of invert sugar, otherwise known as fruit sugar or levulose. Levulose is a form of sugar that occurs widely in nature: for example, honey typically contains about 40% levulose; many wild and cultivated fruits also contain levulose. (That's why it's called fruit sugar.)

For this purpose, levulose is particularly useful because, ounce for ounce, it has nearly twice as much sweetening effect as corn or cane sugar. Sauterne tastes very sweet because the Sauterne yeast tends to reject levulose as a source of energy, and consequently the residual sugar in the wine is mostly levulose.

Dissolved in this levulose syrup is potassium sorbate, which will prevent the wine yeast from budding.

When sweetening a batch of wine, experiment with a sample to find the amount of wine conditioner that will produce just the degree of sweetness you like.

PART TWO

Recipes

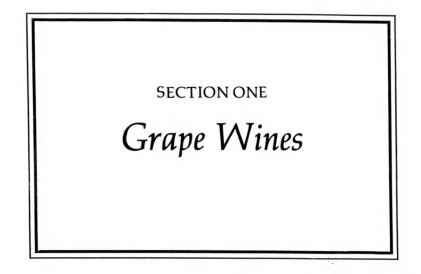

SECTION ONE

Grape Wines

Bardolino

Bardolino, a village in northern Italy, gives its name to the wine produced in the neighborhood. The Bardolino wine is a dark rosé in colour, fruity in character; it is best consumed young.

For initial fermentation	
100 ozs. Italian Premium Red grape concentrate	8 tsps. acid blend
	5 tsps. yeast nutrient
6 cans water	4 Campden tablets
16 ozs. elderberry base	Chianti yeast
5 lbs. white granulated sugar	*To be added later*
	2 ozs. oak chips
	Starting S.G. 1.085

Method

Tie the elderberry base in a nylon straining bag. Start the primary fermentation.

Check S.G. daily. When it falls to 1.030 remove the elderberry base, and rack into secondary fermentor.

In 3 weeks, when S.G. is about 1.000, put the oak chips in a clean secondary fermentor and rack the wine onto them. Top up to the neck.

In 2 months fermentation should be finished, with S.G. between .995 and 1.000. Rack the wine off the oak chips into gallon jugs with fermentation locks or storage valves. Leave in a cool, dark place at least another 4 months.

Bottle and age for 12-18 months.

Yield: 27 26-oz. bottles. Alcohol by volume in finished wine: 11.5%.

Burgundy

Burgundy is a full-bodied, dry red table wine. High-quality French Burgundy is expensive to buy; but some of the California varietal wines, such as Pinot Noir, are good counterparts of the real thing. In the following recipe, oak chips are used to simulate barrel aging.

For initial fermentation	
1 160-oz. can Spanish Red Grape concentrate	1½ ozs. acid blend
	5 Campden tablets
4 cans water	5 tsps. yeast nutrient
3 lbs. white granulated sugar	Burgundy yeast
½ tsp. grape tannin	*To be added later*
	2 ozs. oak chips
	Starting S.G. 1.095

Method

Conduct primary fermentation as usual. When S.G. is 1.030, siphon to secondary fermentor.

When S.G. is 1.010, rack and add the oak chips. After one month, taste the wine; if sufficient oak flavour has developed, rack, and discard the oak chips. If not, taste weekly until the oak flavour is strong enough.

When wine is clear and stable, bottle and age 6 months.

Yield: 30 26-oz. bottles.

Chablis

Chablis is the best-known white Burgundy; the California varietal wine Pinot Chardonnay is its U.S. counterpart. This recipe gives a full-bodied, Chablis-type dry white table wine.

Ingredients

1 160-oz. can Spanish White Grape concentrate	2 ozs. acid blend
4 cans water	5 Campden tablets
3 lbs. white granulated sugar	5 tsps. yeast nutrient
1 tsp. grape tannin	Chablis yeast
	Starting S.G. 1.090-1.095

Method

Conduct primary fermentation as usual. When S.G. is 1.030, siphon to secondary fermentor.

When S.G. is 1.010, rack.

When S.G. is .995, rack again and add 1 Campden tablet per gallon.

When wine is clear and stable, bottle. Age 6 months.

Yield: 30 26-oz. bottles.

Claret

Claret is the English name for red wines from the Bordeaux region of France. Many red wines are sold under this name in North America; but a good claret-type wine will be very dry, and high in tannin and acid content.

For initial fermentation

1 80-oz. can Red Grape concentrate	2 ozs. acid blend
8 cans water	5 Campden tablets
5½ lbs. white granulated sugar	1 oz. yeast nutrient
1½ tsps. grape tannin	Bordeaux or Cabernet yeast
	To be added later
	2 ozs. oak chips
	Starting S.G. 1.085

Method

When S.G. is 1.030, siphon to secondary fermentors.

In 2 to 3 weeks, when S.G. is about .995, rack the wine onto the oak chips.

After 3 months, rack wine off the oak chips into clean secondary fermentors. Make sure they are topped up; use a little water if necessary. Keep under fermentation locks for 4 more months.

If wine is then not perfectly clear, use finings, rack and bottle. Age 6 months.

Yield: 27 26-oz. bottles.

Cream Sherry

Cream sherry is a full-bodied, sweet, rich wine of about 20% alcoholic content, very popular as a dessert or after-dinner wine, also commonly served as an aperitif.

As a general rule, winemakers take elaborate precautions to avoid oxidation – topping-up of fermentors, sulphiting, and so on. Yet, to attain the special sherry flavour, we deliberately let the wine get oxidized! In Spain, the barrels are left only partly full, so that the maturing wine gets ample exposure to air; we imitate this procedure.

Another special feature of Spanish sherry technique is the use of gypsum – calcium sulphate, the mineral from which plaster of Paris is made. It may sound an unlikely ingredient, yet experience has well proved its worth.

For initial fermentation

1 80-oz. can Spanish White Grape concentrate
1 80-oz. can Spanish Fig concentrate *or* 4 lbs. dried white figs, chopped

16 ozs. dried bananas
6 lbs. white granulated sugar
10 80-oz. cans water
1 tsp. grape tannin
1 oz. tartaric acid

6 Campden tablets
3 tsps. yeast energizer *or* Vita-Vin
Sherry yeast starter

To be added later
5 lbs. white sugar
4 ozs. gypsum
    Starting S.G. 1.090

Method

Cut up the bananas before use. Conduct primary fermentation as usual.

When S.G. falls to 1.040, withdraw 4 cups of must, dissolve the extra 5 lbs. sugar, and stir in.

When S.G. again falls to 1.040, strain out the bananas.

Now put half the gypsum in your secondary fermentor (or, if you are using several fermentors, divide the 2 ozs. equally among them).

Siphon the wine into the secondary fermentors; take care to leave the carboy or jugs only 4/5 full, to get ample aeration. Apply fermentation locks.

In 1 month, rack into a clean carboy or jugs; hold the siphon outlet up in the neck of the fermentor, so that the wine splashes, and is again aerated; but this time fill the fermentors up to the neck. Add the rest of the gypsum.

In 3 months, rack. When all fermentation is finished, sweeten to taste and fortify with brandy, 1 or 2 fluid ounces per bottle. Age 1 year.

Yield: 36 26-oz. bottles.

Graves

Graves (*grahv*) is an area in Bordeaux that produces excellent red and white wines, although in the wine trade the regional name is not usually attached to the red. The name Graves Supérieure is usually restricted to white wine of average or better quality. It is a dry white wine of medium body and good bouquet.

Ingredients

1 100-oz. can Italian Premium White Grape concentrate	1 tsp. grape tannin
	2 tsps. acid blend
	4 Campden tablets
6 cans water	1 oz. yeast nutrient
10 ozs. apple concentrate	Graves yeast
1 oz. elderflowers	Starting S.G. 1.090
5 lbs. white granulated sugar	

Method

Start primary fermentation as usual, but without the elderflowers. When fermentation has begun, tie the elderflowers in a fine nylon straining bag and hang it in the fermentor for 12 hours, then remove. *Do not squeeze the bag.*

When S.G. is 1.030, rack to secondary fermentor. Keep fermentor topped up at all times.

When S.G. is 1.000, rack again.

After 2 months, rack again. If the wine is not clear, use finings.

After 4 months, bottle and age 1 year.

Alcohol by volume in finished wine: 12%.

Yield: 27 26-oz. bottles.

Marsala

This wine, somewhat similar to Spanish sherry, originated around the city of Marsala in Sicily. Marsala is the best-known of all Italian fortified wines, and is often used in cooking. The sweet version is the one most commonly seen in North America, but Marsala can also be medium-dry or dry.

For initial fermentation

1 80-oz. can Spanish White Grape concentrate	Sherry yeast starter
8 cans water	*To be added later*
2 ozs. banana powder	3 lbs. white sugar
5 lbs. white granulated sugar	1 bottle Old Smoothy *or* 4 fl. ozs. glycerine
1 lb. dark dried malt extract	1 Noirot yellow brandy extract, ¾ fl. oz.
1 tsp. grape tannin	Wine conditioner (if required)
4 tsps. acid blend	Starting S.G. 1.100
2 tsps. yeast energizer *or* Vita-Vin	

Note: The recipe as printed includes no Campden tablets for the initial fermentation. That's because the Spanish concentrate usually contains enough SO₂. If the concentrate is packaged in plastic, it does contain SO_2. But if it comes in a can, it has no SO_2, so use 4 Campden tablets.

Method

First dissolve the banana powder and 5 lbs. sugar in 1 gallon of warm water; the banana powder will be lumpy, but with stirring will dissolve.

Add the rest of the ingredients and start primary fermentation. Check S.G. daily. When it falls to 1.030, dissolve 2 lbs. of the extra sugar in 4 cups of the wine, and stir in.

When S.G. again falls to 1.030, rack to secondary fermentor. Make sure fermentor is full up to neck; top up with water if necessary.

Check S.G. every other day. When it falls to 1.015, withdraw 4 cups of wine, dissolve the remaining 1 lb. sugar, and return it to the fermentor. This will cause foaming. When foaming stops, make sure fermentor is topped up again.

(If for some reason the fermentation stops before S.G. falls to 1.015, *do not add the extra 1 lb. sugar,* but wait 2 weeks, then rack to a clean fermentor.)

Normally, S.G. should fall to between 1.000 and 1.005 by the time fermentation stops; then rack to a clean fermentor.

Three months later, rack again; make sure fermentor is topped up.

When the wine is clear and stable, siphon into primary fermentor, and add enough wine conditioner to raise S.G. to 1.010. (For this batch of wine, 9 ozs. conditioner will raise S.G. by 5 degrees. For example, if terminal S.G. was 1.000, you would need 18 ozs. conditioner to bring it up to 1.010.)

However, if terminal S.G. is higher than 1.010, *do not* add the wine conditioner, but proceed with the next step.

Gently stir in 1 bottle of Old Smoothy and 1 Noirot Yellow Brandy extract. Bottle and age 6 months or more.

Alcohol by volume in the finished wine is about 14%. *Yield:* 27 26-oz. bottles.

Moselle

Many people consider Moselle the most delicate, fragrant and distinguished of all white wines. It is usually high in acid and has a slight residual sweetness.

For initial fermentation

112 ozs. Spanish White Grape concentrate	5½ U.S. gals. (4⅔ Canadian gals.) water
28 ozs. Mead base *or* 2 lbs. honey	3½ lbs. white sugar
	1½ tsps. grape tannin
	4 tsps. tartaric acid

Bernkastler yeast
1½ tsps. yeast energizer *or*
Vita-Vin

To be added later
1 oz. elderflowers
2 ozs. malic acid

Method

Start the primary fermentation as usual. When fermentation is apparent (this may take 3 to 4 days) tie the elderflowers in a fine nylon straining bag and add them to the must. After 2 days, remove the elderflowers. *Do not squeeze the bag to remove moisture*; if you do, some fine solids will go through the bag, and tend to make the wine cloudy.

When S.G. is 1.040, dissolve the 2 ozs. malic acid in a little wine and stir in.

When S.G. is 1.030, siphon wine to secondary fermentor and attach fermentation locks.

Rack when S.G. is 1.000 (2 to 3 weeks).

Rack again in 3 months, adding 1 teaspoon antioxidant crystals. (This teaspoon is distributed evenly through the entire batch.)

Fine with Serena Finings, following the instructions on the package. When the wine is perfectly clear (about 1 week), rack again.

Check S.G., then sweeten to a S.G. of 1.002 with wine conditioner.

Bottle, and age in a cool, dark place for 8 to 12 months. *Yield*: 36 26-oz. bottles.

Old Brown Sherry

This brown, sweet, full-bodied wine was at one time called East India Sherry, because it was aged in the holds of sailing ships on a voyage from Europe to the East Indies and back.

For initial fermentation

1 30-oz. can White Grape concentrate
16 cans water
1 30-oz. can Fig concentrate *or* 2 lbs. dried white figs, chopped
8 ozs. dried bananas
4 lbs. white granulated sugar
1 lb. dried malt extract
1 tsp. grape tannin
4 ozs. glycerine

10 tsps. tartaric acid
2 Campden tablets
2 tsps. yeast nutrient
2 tsps. yeast energizer
Sherry yeast starter

To be added later
2 lbs. brown sugar
2 ozs. gypsum
White granulated sugar as required
11 stabilizer tablets
36 fl. ozs. brandy (optional)
Starting S.G. 1.090

Method

Begin primary fermentation as usual. When S.G. falls to 1.020 (after 3 or 4 days' active fermentation) take out 4 cups of wine, dissolve the 2 lbs. brown sugar, and stir in.

Two days later, strain out the bananas. Siphon the wine into gallon jugs, putting 2 tsps. of gypsum into each jug. Have each jug only about ⅔ full. Attach fermentation locks.

After 3 weeks, check specific gravity and add white sugar to bring it up to 1.030. (For calculating quantities of sugar required, *see* "Sugar and Specific Gravity", p. 58.

Then put 1 tsp. of gypsum each into clean gallon jugs and rack the wine onto the gypsum. (Use a ½-gal. jug with ½ tsp. of gypsum for any surplus amount.) Top up to necks of jugs with water if necessary. Attach fermentation locks.

After 3 months, check S.G. and again add sugar to bring it up to 1.030.

When the wine is clear and stable, siphon into the primary fermentor; adjust S.G. again to 1.030 (this is meant to be a sweet wine). Crush and add the stabilizer tablets; add, if desired, the 36 fl. ozs. brandy, and stir in.

Bottle and age for 18 to 24 months.

Yield: 21 26-oz. bottles.

Quinine-Flavoured Aperitif

The word "aperitif" is derived from the Latin *aperire*, meaning to open. Aperitifs are meant to be taken at the beginning of a meal, to stimulate the appetite. The well-known aperitifs Dubonnet, Byrrh and Campari are quinined wines.

Quinine, extracted from the bark of the South American cinchona tree, was first used as a remedy for malaria, and later came to be appreciated for its incisive, appetizing flavour. The quinined wines are now popularly served on the rocks, or with soda.

The following recipe produces a high-alcohol wine which is then sweetened, fortified and flavoured with cinchona essence to produce a tangy, bitter flavour similar to that of Dubonnet.

For initial fermentation	*To be added later*
1 80-oz. can Spanish Red Grape concentrate	Approximately 1½ lbs. white granulated sugar
4 cans water	1 tsp. yeast energizer
1½ lbs. white granulated sugar	
¼ tsp. grape tannin	*For final flavouring*
1 oz. acid blend	1½ tsps. cinchona essence
3 Campden tablets	15 fl. ozs. brandy
2 tsps. yeast energizer	15 fl. ozs. sugar syrup (2 parts sugar to 1 part water)
All-purpose wine yeast	Starting S.G. 1.095 to 1.100

Method

Begin primary fermentation as usual. When S.G. is 1.030, dissolve and add 8 ozs. extra sugar. Siphon into gallon jugs and attach fermentation locks.

When S.G. is 1.010, dissolve and add 8 ozs. more sugar, divided equally between the jugs.

When S.G. is 1.000 and fermentation is still apparent,

add another 8 ozs. sugar, plus an additional tsp. of yeast energizer to aid fermentation.

As long as fermentation continues, add small amounts of extra sugar in stages—say 1 oz. per gal. at a time. In this way you can bring the wine up to 18% alcohol by volume.

When all fermentation has ceased, rack the wine and store for 2 or 3 months, until it is clear.

Now for the final flavouring. Rack into clean jugs. The quantity of cinchona essence indicated will suit many palates, but some people might find it too much. So I would recommend that, when making your first batch, you use only half the amount of cinchona essence, that is, ¾ tsp; mix thoroughly, and taste to see if that's enough for you. If so, don't add the rest.

Mix the cinchona essence with the brandy first (it won't dissolve in water), add the sugar syrup, and distribute the mixture equally among the jugs.

The cinchona essence may cause the wine to become cloudy, so store it for 1 month before bottling. Age 6 months.

Yield: 15 26-oz. bottles.

Ruby Port

Port is a sweet, fortified wine from the Douro valley of northern Portugal. Ruby Port is fairly young in contrast to Tawny Port, which has spent more time in oak; many people enjoy its bright red colour and fresh, fruity flavour.

For initial fermentation

1 80-oz. can Spanish Red Grape concentrate
8 cans water
16 ozs. elderberry base
2 ozs. banana powder
7 lbs. white granulated sugar
1 lb. light dried malt extract
1 oz. acid blend
2 tsps. yeast energizer *or* Vita-Vin

Port wine yeast starter

To be added later
2 lbs. white granulated sugar
1 package all-purpose wine yeast
Wine conditioner as required
12 fl. ozs. brandy (optional)
Starting S.G. 1.095

Method

First dissolve the 7 lbs. sugar and the banana powder in 1 gal. of warm water; the banana powder will be lumpy, but with stirring will dissolve.

Put the elderberry base in a nylon straining bag and tie the neck with string. Add the rest of the ingredients and start the primary fermentation.

Keep watch on the fermentation. Port yeast may be rather sluggish to act, particularly if it is not warm enough; 75°F. (24°C.) is suitable. If fermentation stops, add a package of good, all-purpose wine yeast such as Andovin, and stir in.

Check S.G. daily. When it falls to 1.030, dissolve the extra 2 lbs. sugar in some of the must, and stir in. If the Andovin was not used before, stir it in now.

When S.G. falls again to 1.030, remove the elderberries, squeezing out the bag. Siphon the wine into secondary fermentors.

When the S.G. is 1.010, rack and top up. In 3 months, rack again and top up. Store in a dark place at 50°-65°F. (10°-18°C.) until the wine is clear and stable.

Before bottling, check S.G. and add enough wine conditioner to bring it up to 1.015. (If S.G. is higher than 1.015, *do not* add wine conditioner.)

You can bottle the wine as it is, at about 14% alcohol by volume; or, if you wish, add the brandy to fortify it.

Yield: 27 26-oz. bottles.

Sauterne

This recipe produces a Sauterne-type sweet white wine, full-bodied, fragrant, and with 14% to 15% alcohol by volume – very popular with people who don't care for dry wines.

For initial fermentation

1 100-oz. can Hidalgo White Grape concentrate
7 cans water
8 ozs. dried bananas
8 lbs. white granulated sugar
2 ozs. dried elderflowers
8 fl. ozs. glycerine
1 tsp. grape tannin
1 oz. acid blend
5 antioxidant tablets
2 tsps. yeast energizer
Sauterne yeast starter

To be added later
1 lb. white granulated sugar
5 Campden tablets
Wine conditioner to taste

Method

Cut up the bananas before use. Wait until primary fermentation is well started, then tie the elderflowers in a piece of cheesecloth or a nylon straining bag and add to the must. On the third day of active fermentation, remove the elderflowers. *Do not squeeze the bag to remove moisture.*

When S.G. falls to 1.040, strain out the bananas with a plastic strainer, stir in the extra 1 lb. sugar and siphon into secondary fermentors.

When secondary fermentation has stopped, rack again and add the other 5 Campden tablets.

When the wine is clear, sweeten to taste and stabilize with wine conditioner. Bottle and age 6 months.

Yield: 30 26-oz. bottles.

Sparkling Rosé

Ingredients

1 80-oz. can White Grape concentrate	1 tsp. grape tannin
8½ cans water	3 ozs. acid blend
30 ozs. Red Grape concentrate	5 Campden tablets
5 lbs. white granulated sugar	1 oz. yeast nutrient
	All-purpose wine yeast
	Starting S.G. 1.085
	Starting acid level .7%

Method

Proceed in the usual way. When the wine is clear and stable, use one of the sparkling-wine processes described in this book or in *The Art of Making Wine*.

Note that this recipe also produces an excellent still rosé. You can bottle it dry as it is, or sweeten it with wine conditioner, with sugar syrup and stabilizer, or by pasteurization.

Yield: 30 26-oz. bottles.

Tarragona Port

From Tarragona, a city and province on the Mediterranean coast of Spain, comes the sweet, fortified red wine that is Spain's answer to the Port of Portugal.

For initial fermentation

1 80-oz. can Spanish Red Grape concentrate	2 ozs. acid blend
8 cans water	3 Campden tablets
1 lb. dried bananas	4 tsps. yeast nutrient
6 ozs. dried elderberries	2 tsps. yeast energizer
1 lb. white granulated sugar	Port or Malaga yeast starter
6 lbs. Demerara sugar	
1 lb. dried malt extract	*To be added later*
1 Noirot Yellow Brandy flavour, ¾ fl. oz.	White granulated sugar as required
½ tsp. grape tannin	1 Noirot Yellow Brandy flavour, ¾ fl. oz. *or* 10 fl. ozs. brandy
8 fl. ozs. glycerine	15 stabilizer tablets.

Note: If dried bananas are not available, substitute 4 ozs. banana powder, or 3 lbs. fresh bananas.

Method

Mix the first batch of ingredients in primary fermentor, except yeast, dried bananas, the 1 lb. sugar and 1½ cups water.

Cut up dried bananas, add the 1 lb. white sugar and 1 cup water. Simmer on low heat for 10 minutes, stirring to prevent burning. Remove from the heat, add ½ cup cold water, stir and add to the must in primary fermentor. Then start primary fermentation as usual.

After 2 days of active fermentation, dissolve and add 2 lbs. more white sugar.

When S.G. is 1.030 (about 3 more days), strain out

bananas and elderberries. Siphon into gallon jugs and attach fermentation locks.

After 2 weeks, check S.G. and, if necessary, add sugar to bring it up again to 1.030. (For calculating quantities of sugar, see "Sugar and Specific Gravity" in Part I.)

After 3 weeks, rack into clean jugs, check S.G., and again add sugar to bring it up to 1.030.

Rack again in 3 months and if necessary add sugar to bring S.G. up to 1.025. (But if S.G. is still 1.025 or over, add no more sugar.)

Wait till all fermentation has stopped. Then, if wine is not clear, fine with Sparkolloid.

When wine is clear, rack into primary fermentor. If necessary, add sugar to bring S.G. up again to 1.025. Crush the stabilizer tablets, dissolve in a small amount of wine and stir in.

Add the brandy extract and stir well to blend. (This second brandy extract is in addition to the one used in primary fermentation.) If you prefer, use brandy instead of the extract.

Bottle and store in a cool place for 18 to 24 months.

Yield: 27 26-oz. bottles.

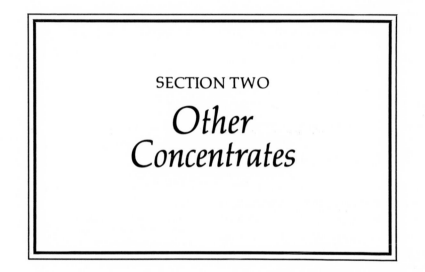

SECTION TWO

Other Concentrates

Apricot Dessert Wine

This recipe produces a rich, sweet dessert wine, similar in flavour to apricot brandy.

For initial fermentation

19 ozs. Apricot wine base
30 ozs. White Grape

9 30-oz. cans water
4 lbs. white granulated
  sugar
1 Noirot Apricot Brandy
  flavour, ¾ fl. oz.
4 fl. ozs. glycerine
¼ tsp. grape tannin
1 tsp. pectic enzyme
  powder

4 tsps. acid blend
3 Campden tablets
2 tsps. yeast nutrient
All-purpose wine yeast

To be added later
Sugar syrup (2 parts sugar
  to 1 part water)
1½ lbs. sugar
1 Noirot Apricot Brandy
  flavour, ¾ fl. oz.
6 stabilizer tablets
  Starting S.G. 1.100

Method

Start primary fermentation as usual. When S.G. falls to 1.050, strain out apricot pulp with a plastic strainer.

When S.G. is 1.030, siphon to secondary fermentors.

Rack in 3 weeks and top up with sugar syrup.

Rack again in 3 months.

When S.G. is 1.000 and wine is clear, rack again, carefully, to avoid splashing. Dissolve the extra 1½ lbs. sugar and stir in. Crush the stabilizer tablets, dissolve in a little wine, and stir in with the second apricot brandy flavour. (Or, if you prefer a real fortified wine, you can substitute 26 fl. ozs. brandy for the 6 stabilizer tablets.)

Store in gallon jugs for 2 weeks before bottling. Age in bottle 2 months.

Yield: 12 26-oz. bottles.

Blackberry Dessert Wine

This is a strong, sweet dessert wine, similar in flavour to blackberry brandy.

For initial fermentation

1 100-oz. can Blackberry
  wine base
3½ cans water
30 ozs. Red Grape
  concentrate
4 lbs. white sugar
2 lbs. Demerara sugar
2 ozs. dried elderberries
1 Noirot Blackberry
  flavour, ¾ fl. oz.
8 fl. ozs. glycerine
1½ tsps. pectic enzyme
  powder

6 tsps. acid blend
3 Campden tablets
3 tsps. yeast nutrient
All-purpose wine yeast

To be added later
Sugar syrup (2 parts sugar
  to 1 part water)
2 lbs. white sugar
1 Noirot Blackberry
  flavour, ¾ fl. oz.
9 stabilizer tablets
  Starting S.G. 1.110 to
  1.115

Method

Tie the blackberry wine base and the dried elderberries in a nylon straining bag; start fermentation as usual.

When S.G. is 1.040 (about 3 or 4 days), strain out the fruit pulp and elderberries and siphon to a secondary fermentor.

After 3 weeks, rack and top up with sugar syrup.

Rack again after 3 months.

When S.G. is 1.000 and the wine is clear and stable, rack again to the primary fermentor (avoid splashing). Dissolve the extra 2 lbs. sugar and stir in. Crush the stabilizer tablets, dissolve in a little wine, and stir in with the second blackberry flavour.

Store in gallon jugs for 2 weeks, then bottle. Age in bottle for 2 months.

Yield: 18 26-oz. bottles.

Cherry Dessert Wine

This is a rich, sweet dessert wine with a pronounced cherry flavour; it is similar to a well-known Danish cherry wine.

For initial fermentation

1 19-oz. can Cherry Wine base
1 30-oz. can Red Grape concentrate
9 30-oz. cans water
1 Noirot Cherry Brandy flavour, ¾ fl. oz.
2 ozs. dried elderberries
2 lbs. Demerara sugar
1¾ lbs. white granulated sugar
4 fl. ozs. glycerine
4 tsps. acid blend
3 Campden tablets
2 tsps. yeast nutrient
Wine yeast

To be added later

Sugar syrup (2 parts sugar to 1 part water)
1 Cherry Brandy flavour, ¾ fl. oz.
1 Noirot Almond flavour, ¾ fl. oz.
1½ lbs. white granulated sugar
6 stabilizer tablets

Starting S.G. 1.110

Method

Begin fermentation as usual. When S.G. is 1.050, strain out elderberries and cherry pulp with a plastic strainer.

When S.G. is 1.030, rack to secondary fermentor.

Rack again in 3 weeks, and top up with sugar syrup.

Rack again after 3 months.

When the wine is clear and S.G. is 1.000, rack into the primary fermentor (avoid splashing).

Dissolve the stabilizer tablets, plus the extra 1½ lbs. sugar, in some of the wine, and stir in. Also stir in the second cherry brandy flavour and the almond flavour.

Store in gallon jugs for 2 weeks, then bottle and age at least 2 months.

Yield: 12 26-oz. bottles.

Elderberry Wine

This recipe produces a dry red wine; if you prefer a sweet wine, see the note below.

Ingredients

15 ozs. Elderberry
  concentrate
6 lbs. white granulated
  sugar
18 pints (U.S.) *or* 15 pints
  (Canadian) water

1 tsp. pectic enzyme
  powder
8 tsps. acid blend
2 Campden tablets
2 tsps. yeast nutrient
All-purpose wine yeast
  Starting S.G. 1.095

Method

Conduct primary and secondary fermentation as usual. When the wine is clear and stable, it may be bottled as a dry wine.

  Yield: 12 26-oz. bottles.

Note: For a sweet wine, sweeten to taste with wine conditioner; or use sugar syrup to taste, plus 6 wine stabilizer tablets.

Gooseberry Wine

Gooseberry concentrate produces a lovely white wine of delicate character and flavour. It is suitable for making white table wines, sparkling wines and light social wines; blended with coloured fruit such as red grapes or black-berries, it yields a delicious rosé.

  Note that processing methods are identical for all four wines described below (except for the final stages of Gooseberry Champagne) so, to save space, instructions are printed once only, after the fourth recipe.

Dry White Gooseberry Wine

1 100-oz. can Gooseberry
  wine base
6 cans water
13 lbs. corn sugar *or* 10 lbs.
  white granulated sugar
2½ tsps. pectic enzyme
  powder

½ tsp. grape tannin
7 tsps. acid blend
4 Campden tablets
5 tsps. yeast nutrient
Hock or Chablis yeast
  Starting S.G. 1.090

Sweet Gooseberry Wine

1 100-oz. can Gooseberry
  wine base
6 cans water
14 lbs. corn sugar *or* 11 lbs.
  white granulated sugar
2½ tsps. pectic enzyme
  powder

powder
½ tsp. grape tannin
7 tsps. acid blend
4 Campden tablets
5 tsps. yeast energizer
All-purpose wine yeast
  Starting S.G. 1.100

Gooseberry Rosé

1 100-oz. can Gooseberry
  wine base
1 10-oz. can Red Grape
  concentrate or 1 16-oz. can
  Blackberry wine base
6 100-oz. cans water
11 lbs. corn sugar *or* 9 lbs.
  white granulated sugar

2½ tsps. pectic enzyme
  powder
½ tsp. grape tannin
7 tsps. acid blend
4 Campden tablets
5 tsps. yeast nutrient
All-purpose wine yeast
  Starting S.G. 1.085

Gooseberry Champagne

1 100-oz. can Gooseberry wine base
6 cans water
12 lbs. corn sugar *or* 9½ lbs. white granulated sugar
2½ tsps. pectic enzyme powder
½ tsp. grape tannin
4 Campden tablets
5 tsps. yeast nutrient
Champagne yeast
Starting S.G. 1.085

General Method

Tie the gooseberry wine base into a straining bag and begin primary fermentation as usual.

In 4 to 5 days, when S.G. is 1.030, remove the straining bag, squeezing out surplus juice. Siphon the wine into secondary fermentors.

In 2 to 3 weeks, when S.G. is 1.010 to 1.000, rack.

Rack again in 2 months.

When wine is clear and stable, bottle it.

Yield: 15 26-oz. bottles.

Sweetening

For the sweet wine, sweeten to taste by one of the methods previously described in this book.

Sparkling Wine

For the gooseberry champagne, use one of the methods described in *The Art of Making Wine* or in Part I of this book.

Note that the Gooseberry Rosé also makes an excellent sparkling wine.

Liebfraumilch

Liebfraumilch is a light white wine with just a hint of sweetness — one of the best-known German wines in North America. This recipe, using Apricot wine base, yields the delicate taste and bouquet of a good Liebfraumilch, with just the right degree of residual sweetness.

Ingredients

1 100-oz. can Apricot wine base
7 cans water
16 fl. ozs. Rose Hip purée
13 lbs. white granulated sugar
1 oz. elderflowers
2 tsps. grape tannin
2 tsps. pectic enzyme powder
3½ ozs. acid blend
5 Campden tablets
1 oz. yeast nutrient
Liebfraumilch yeast
Starting S.G. 1.085

Method

Begin the primary fermentation as usual, with all ingredients except the elderflowers. When the fermentation is well started, tie the elderflowers in a nylon straining bag and hang it in the must. Remove the bag after 2 days; *do not squeeze the bag to expel moisture.*

When S.G. is 1.030, strain out fruit pulp and rack into secondary fermentors.

In 2 to 3 weeks, when S.G. is about 1.000, rack.

Rack again in 3 months.

When the wine is clear and stable, bottle. Age in a cool, dark place for 9 months.

Yield: 30 26-oz. bottles.

Passionfruit Wine

This recipe produces a medium-dry, white dinner wine.

Ingredients

1 100-oz. can Passionfruit concentrate	3 tsps. pectic enzyme powder
8½ cans water	1 tsp. acid blend
16 lbs. white granulated sugar	6 Campden tablets
1 tsp. grape tannin	1 oz. yeast nutrient
	All-purpose wine yeast
	Starting S.G. 1.090

Method

Conduct primary and secondary fermentations as usual. When the wine is clear and stable, bottle it.

For a sweet wine, sweeten to taste by one of the methods described in Part I.

Yield: 36 26-oz. bottles.

Peach Dessert Wine

This is a rich, sweet dessert wine, similar in flavour to peach brandy.

For initial fermentation

1 19-oz. can Peach Wine base	4 tsps. acid blend
1 30-oz. can White Grape concentrate	3 Campden tablets
9 30-oz. cans water	2 tsps. yeast nutrient
4 lbs. white granulated sugar	All-purpose wine yeast
1 Noirot Peach Brandy flavour, ¾ fl. oz.	*To be added later*
¼ tsp. grape tannin	Sugar syrup (2 parts sugar to 1 part water)
4 fl. ozs. glycerine	1½ lbs. white granulated sugar
1 tsp. pectic enzyme powder	1 Noirot Peach Brandy flavour, ¾ fl. oz.
	6 stabilizer tablets
	Starting S.G. 1.100

Method

Conduct primary and secondary fermentation as usual. Keep secondary fermentors topped up, as necessary, with sugar syrup.

When wine is clear and S.G. is 1.000, rack it back into the primary fermentor, carefully, with no splashing.

Dissolve the extra 1½ lbs. sugar and stir in. Crush,

dissolve and stir in the stabilizer tablets; add the second Peach Brandy flavour.

Store in gallon jugs for 2 weeks more, then bottle. Age 2 months or more.

Yield: 12 26-oz. bottles.

Plum Dessert Wine

This is a rich, sweet dessert wine, similar in flavour to plum brandy or prunelle.

For initial fermentation

1 19-oz. can Plum Wine
  base
1 30-oz. can Red Grape
  concentrate
9 30-oz. cans water
4 lbs. white granulated
  sugar
1 Noirot Prunelle flavour,
  ¾ fl. oz.
2 ozs. dried elderberries
4 fl. ozs. glycerine
1 tsp. pectic enzyme
  powder

4 tsps. acid blend
3 Campden tablets
2 tsps. yeast nutrient
All-purpose wine yeast

To be added later
Sugar syrup (2 parts sugar
  to 1 part water)
1½ lbs. white granulated
  sugar
1 Noirot Prunelle flavour,
  ¾ fl. oz.
6 stabilizer tablets
  Starting S.G. 1.100

Method
Begin primary fermentation as usual. When S.G. falls to 1.050, strain out plum pulp and elderberries.

When S.G. is 1.030, siphon into secondary fermentors.

When wine is clear and S.G. is 1.000, rack it back into the primary fermentor, carefully, with no splashing.

Dissolve the extra 1½ lbs. sugar, and stir in. Crush, dissolve and stir in the stabilizer tablets; add the second Prunelle flavour.

Store in gallon jugs for 2 weeks more, then bottle. Age 2 months or more.

Yield: 12 26-oz. bottles.

Sparkling Pash

Here is a light, white sparkling wine made from passion-fruit concentrate; it is similar to cider in alcoholic content, and is meant to be made and consumed within 6 months.

For initial fermentation

1 100-oz. can Passionfruit
  concentrate
11½ cans water 14 lbs.
14 lbs. white granulated
  sugar
1 tsp. grape tannin
4 tsps. pectic enzyme
  powder
2 tsps. acid blend
8 Campden tablets

8 tsps. yeast nutrient
All-purpose wine yeast

To be added later
1 lb. white granulated sugar
1 package all-purpose wine
  yeast
1 tsp. antioxidant crystals
  (sodium erythorbate)
  Starting S.G. 1.060

Conduct primary and secondary fermentation as usual.

When the wine is clear and stable, siphon into primary fermentor. Dissolve the extra 1 lb. sugar and the wine yeast in a pint of the wine, and stir in. Stir in the anti-oxidant crystals.

Siphon into beer or pop bottles and close with crown caps.

Store upright for 1 month; the wine is then ready to chill and serve.

Yield: 106 12-oz. bottles.

SECTION THREE

Country Wines

Country wines have sometimes been underrated by experienced winemakers; that's because, in bygone days, they were often made so badly, using a miscellany of fruits or vegetables, often with excessive sugar, fermented with bread-yeast to yield a low-alcohol beverage either syrupy-sweet or vinegary.

This liquid – if the bottles didn't explode first – was finally served, cloudy, off a deep deposit of yeast and autolyzed vegetable matter. Admittedly, it was cheap; children liked the flavour of the super-sweet kinds; and, if you swallowed enough of the stuff, it would make you drunk – provided it didn't make you sick first.

Yet I confidently say that, made as described here, country wines deserve a place on anyone's table.

There is no need in this book to give detailed processing instructions for these wines. For some of them, one or two special steps are needed; those are described in their place. Here are a few general points.

All fruit or vegetables should be cut up or crushed; large fruit-stones such as peach, apricot and plum should be removed.

For recipes where fruit or vegetable pulp is present, you can save labour by putting the pulp into a large mesh bag for the primary fermentation; then its eventual removal is easier.

Most of these recipes will give you a dry wine. For sweet wines, don't add extra sugar when fermenting; sweeten to taste, when bottling, with wine conditioner, or with sugar syrup plus 2 stabilizer tablets per U.S. gallon, 3 per Canadian (imperial) gallon.

You can multiply the suggested recipes to make larger volumes of these wines.

For a radically different approach to this branch of the winemaker's art, you can try the procedure described under "Country Wines" in Part I of this book, and produce a whole range of additional recipes.

Banana Wine

Ingredients	U.S. Measure	Canadian Measure
Bananas	3 lbs.	4 lbs.
Sugar	2½ lbs.	3 lbs.
Water	1 gal.	1 gal.
Grape tannin	¼ tsp.	¼ tsp.
Acid blend	3 tsps.	4 tsps.
Campden tablets	1	2
Yeast nutrient	1 tsp.	1 tsp.
Wine yeast	1 package	1 package

Starting S.G. 1.095 to 1.100

Method

Bring some of the water to a boil and simmer the bananas for half an hour. Strain, allow to cool, and use only this liquid with the rest of the ingredients.

Beet Wine

Ingredients	U.S. Measure	Canadian Measure
Beets	3 lbs.	4 lbs.
Sugar	2½ lbs.	3 lbs.
Water	1 gal.	1 gal.
Grape tannin	¼ tsp.	¼ tsp.
Acid blend	2 tsps.	3 tsps.
Campden tablets	1	2
Yeast nutrient	1 tsp.	1 tsp.
Wine yeast	1 package	1 package

Starting S.G. 1.095 to 1.100

Method

Boil the beets until they are soft, peel and cut up before putting them in the must.

Birch Sap Wine

Ingredients	U.S. Measure	Canadian Measure
Birch sap	1 gal.	1 gal.
Raisins	1 lb.	1 lb.
Sugar	1½ lbs.	2 lbs.
Grape tannin	¼ tsp.	¼ tsp.
Acid blend	4 tsps.	5 tsps.
Campden tablets	1	2
Yeast nutrient	1 tsp.	1 tsp.
Wine yeast	1 package	1 package

Starting S.G. 1.090

Method

Tap the trees in March, when the sap begins to rise; but don't tap very young trees. Be sure to plug the holes afterwards.

Instead of the 1 lb. raisins you can, if you like, use 10 fl. ozs. white grape concentrate.

Carrot Wine

Ingredients	U.S. Measure	Canadian Measure
Carrots	3 lbs.	4 lbs.
Raisins	1 lb.	1 lb.
Sugar	2 lbs.	2½ lbs.
Water	1 gal.	1 gal.
Grape tannin	¼ tsp.	¼ tsp.
Acid blend	3 tsps.	4 tsps.
Campden tablets	1	2
Yeast energizer		
or Vita-Vin	½ tsp.	½ tsp.
Wine yeast	1 package	1 package
Starting S.G. 1.095 to 1.100		

Method
Peel and boil the carrots in some of the water until they are soft; strain, and use this liquid with the rest of the ingredients.

Citrus Champagne

Ingredients	U.S. Measure	Canadian Measure
Oranges	2	3
Lemons	2	3
Raisins	½ lb.	½ lb.
Sugar	2 lbs.	2½ lbs.
Water	1 gal.	1 gal.
Campden tablets	1	2
Yeast nutrient	1 tsp.	1 tsp.
Wine yeast	1 package	1 package
Starting S.G. 1.090		

Method
Peel and cut up the oranges and lemons before fermentation.

Check S.G. regularly. When if falls to 1.005, siphon into Champagne bottles or pop bottles; cork or cap, and store upright for 3 weeks.

Elderberry Wine

Ingredients	U.S. Measure	Canadian Measure
Elderberries	3 lbs.	4 lbs.
Sugar	2½ lbs.	3 lbs.
Water	1 gal.	1 gal.
Acid blend	1 tsp.	2 tsps.
Campden tablets	1	2
Yeast nutrient	1 tsp.	1 tsp.
Wine yeast	1 package	1 package

Starting S.G. 1.095 to 1.100

Fresh Fig Wine

Ingredients	U.S. Measure	Canadian Measure
Figs	4 lbs.	6 lbs.
Sugar	2 lbs.	2½ lbs.
Water	1 gal.	1 gal.
Grape tannin	¼ tsp.	¼ tsp.
Pectic enzyme	½ tsp.	½ tsp.

Ingredients	U.S. Measure	Canadian Measure
Acid blend	3 tsps.	4 tsps.
Campden tablets	1	2
Yeast nutrient	1 tsp.	1 tsp.
Wine yeast	1 package	1 package

Starting S.G. 1.095 to 1.100

Note: The fig is a low-acid, high-sugar fruit of low flavour intensity; therefore fig wine is an exception to the general rule on fruit quantities.

Grapefruit Wine

Ingredients	U.S. Measure	Canadian Measure
Grapefruit	5	6
Sugar	2½ lbs.	3 lbs.
Water	1 gal.	1 gal.
Grape tannin	¼ tsp.	¼ tsp.
Campden tablets	1	2
Yeast nutrient	1 tsp.	1 tsp.
Wine yeast	1 package	1 package

Starting S.G. 1.095

Method
Peel the grapefruit and chop up the pulp.

Mead

Mead, or honey wine, is probably the oldest alcoholic beverage. Until the 18th century, sugar was a costly rarity, and honey was the most commonly used sweetening agent.

In some societies, magical and therapeutic properties were ascribed to honey. Mead was supposed to be an aphrodisiac; the word "honeymoon" is derived from the old custom of drinking honey wine during the celebrations following a wedding.

The two recipes given below use other ingredients—grape concentrate and orange juice—in addition to honey, and have the advantage that they yield a faster-maturing mead than that made with honey alone.

Melomel and Pyment are the original, old-time names of these mead variants. I can't promise that they'll produce any aphrodisiac effects, but I can guarantee you a beverage fit for a wedding feast, or any other festive occasion.

Melomel

Ingredients	U.S. Measure	Canadian Measure
Honey	3 lbs.	3 lbs.
Frozen orange juice	2 6-oz. cans	2 6-oz. cans
Water	1.2 gals.	1 gal.
Grape tannin	¼ tsp.	¼ tsp.
Acid blend	2 tsps.	2 tsps.
Campden tablets	2	2
Yeast energizer	½ tsp.	½ tsp.
Wine yeast	1 package	1 package
Starting S.G. 1.090		

Method
Instead of the 2 cans of frozen orange juice you can, if you like, substitute 50 fl. ozs. fresh orange juice, or 12 fl. ozs. non-frozen orange concentrate with SO_2, which will probably be cheaper.

It's best to use a bland, light-coloured honey.

Process as with other country wines, and age 3 to 6 months.

Yield: 6 26-oz. bottles.

Pyment

Ingredients

4 lbs. honey
1 30-oz. can Spanish White Grape concentrate
9 cans water
½ tsp. grape tannin

1 oz. acid blend
4 Campden tablets
1 tsp. yeast energizer
All-purpose wine yeast

Method
Process as for Melomel.
  Yield: 12 26-oz. bottles.

Sweet Mead
Both the above recipes will yield a dry mead. For sweet mead, sweeten to taste and stabilize with wine conditioner at the time of bottling.

Mulberry Wine

Ingredients	U.S. Measure	Canadian Measure
Mulberries	4 lbs.	5 lbs.
Sugar	2 lbs.	3 lbs.
Water	1 gal.	1 gal.
Pectic enzyme	½ tsp.	½ tsp.
Acid blend	1 tsp.	1 tsp.
Campden tablets	1	2
Yeast nutrient	1 tsp.	1 tsp.
Wine yeast	1 package	1 package

Starting S.G. 1.095

Note: The mulberry is a low-acid fruit; like the fig, it is an exception to the general rule for fruit quantities.

Oregon Grape Wine

Ingredients	U.S. Measure	Canadian Measure
Oregon grapes	2½ lbs.	3 lbs.
Raisins	1 lb.	1 lb.
Sugar	2½ lbs.	3 lbs.
Water	1 gal.	1 gal.
Pectic enzyme	½ tsp.	½ tsp.
Acid blend	½ tsp.	1 tsp.

Ingredients	U.S. Measure	Canadian Measure
Campden tablets	1	2
Yeast nutrient	1 tsp.	1 tsp.
Wine yeast	1 package	1 package
Starting S.G. 1.100		

Parsley Wine

Ingredients	U.S. Measure	Canadian Measure
Parsley	1 lb.	1 lb.
Orange juice	9 fl. ozs.	12 fl. ozs.
Lemon juice	3 fl. ozs.	4 fl. ozs.
Sugar	2½ lbs.	3 lbs.
Water	1 gal.	1 gal.
Grape tannin	¼ tsp.	¼ tsp.
Campden tablets	1	2
Yeast nutrient	1 tsp.	1 tsp.
Wine yeast	1 package	1 package
Starting S.G. 1.095		

Method

Boil some of the water and pour it over the parsley. Leave it overnight and strain. Use the liquid with the rest of the ingredients.

Parsnip Wine

Ingredients	U.S. Measure	Canadian Measure
Parsnips	3 lbs.	4 lbs.
Raisins	½ lb.	½ lb.
Sugar	2½ lbs.	3 lbs.
Water	1 gal.	1 gal.
Grape tannin	¼ tsp.	¼ tsp.
Acid blend	2 tsps.	3 tsps.
Campden tablets	1	2
Yeast nutrient	1 tsp.	1 tsp.
Wine yeast	1 package	1 package
Starting S.G. 1.095 to 1.100		

Method

Peel the parsnips and boil them in some of the water until they are soft. Strain and use this liquid with the rest of the ingredients.

Note that you can, if you wish, omit the raisins and substitute 10 fl. ozs. white grape concentrate.

Pineapple Wine

Ingredients	U.S. Measure	Canadian Measure
Pineapples	2 lbs.	3 lbs.
Sugar	2½ lbs.	3 lbs.
Water	1 gal.	1 gal.
Grape tannin	¼ tsp.	¼ tsp.
Acid blend	½ tsp.	½ tsp.
Campden tablets	1	2
Yeast nutrient	1 tsp.	1 tsp.
Wine yeast	1 package	1 package
Starting S.G. 1.095		

Method
Peel and chop the pineapples.

Pumpkin Wine

Ingredients	U.S. Measure	Canadian Measure
Pumpkin	3 lbs.	4 lbs.
Raisins	½ lb.	½ lb.
Sugar	2½ lbs.	3 lbs.
Water	1 gal.	1 gal.
Grape tannin	¼ tsp.	¼ tsp.
Acid blend	3 tsps.	4 tsps.
Campden tablets	1	2
Yeast nutrient	1 tsp.	1 tsp.
Wine yeast	1 package	1 package
Starting S.G. 1.095 to 1.100		

Method
Peel and chop the pumpkin.

Note that you can, if you prefer, omit the raisins and substitute 10 fl. ozs. white grape concentrate.

Quince Wine

Ingredients	U.S. Measure	Canadian Measure
Quinces	3 lbs.	4 lbs.
Sugar	2½ lbs.	3 lbs.
Water	1 gal.	1 gal.
Pectic enzyme	½ tsp.	½ tsp.
Acid blend	½ tsp.	1 tsp.
Campden tablets	1	2
Yeast nutrient	1 tsp.	1 tsp.
Wine yeast	1 package	1 package

Starting S.G. 1.095 to 1.100

Method
Chop up the quinces.

Red Currant Wine

Ingredients	U.S. Measure	Canadian Measure
Red currants	2 lbs.	3 lbs.

Ingredients	U.S. Measure	Canadian Measure
Sugar	2½ lbs.	3 lbs.
Water	1 gal.	1 gal.
Pectic enzyme	½ tsp.	½ tsp.
Campden tablets	1	2
Yeast nutrient	1 tsp.	1 tsp.
Wine yeast	1 package	1 package

Starting S.G. 1.095 to 1.100

Rice Wine or Saki

Ingredients	U.S. Measure	Canadian Measure
Rice	2 lbs.	2 lbs.
Raisins	1 lb.	1 lb.
Sugar	2½ lbs.	3 lbs.
Water	1 gal.	1 gal.
Acid blend	4 tsps.	5 tsps.
Campden tablets	1	2
Yeast nutrient	1 tsp.	1 tsp.
Wine yeast	1 package	1 package

Starting S.G. 1.100 to 1.005

Note: The rice in this recipe has little more than psychological value to the winemaker. It contributes little or nothing to the wine because wine yeast cannot convert raw rice to alcohol.

Rose Hip Wine

Ingredients	U.S. Measure	Canadian Measure
Rose hips	2 lbs.	3 lbs.
Sugar	2½ lbs.	3 lbs.
Water	1 gal.	1 gal.
Pectic enzyme	½ tsp.	½ tsp.
Acid blend	1 tsp.	2 tsps.
Campden tablets	1	2
Yeast energizer *or* Vita-Vin	½ tsp.	½ tsp.
Wine yeast	1 package	1 package
Starting S.G. 1.095		

Method

Gather rose hips after the first frost and crush them. Boil some of the water, pour it over the crushed hips and leave overnight. Next day add to the rest of the ingredients.

Rose Petal Wine

Ingredients	U.S. Measure	Canadian Measure
Rose petals	8 cups	10 cups
Sugar	2 lbs.	2½ lbs.
Lemon juice	3 fl. ozs.	4 fl. ozs.
Water	1 gal.	1 gal.
Grape tannin	¼ tsp.	¼ tsp.
Campden tablets	1	2
Yeast energizer *or* Vita-Vin	½ tsp.	½ tsp.
Wine yeast	1 package	1 package
Starting S.G. 1.090 to 1.095		

Rowanberry or Mountain Ash Wine

Ingredients	U.S. Measure	Canadian Measure
Rowanberries	2½ lbs.	3 lbs.
Raisins	½ lb.	½ lb.

Ingredients	U.S. Measure	Canadian Measure
Sugar	2½ lbs.	3 lbs.
Water	1 gal.	1 gal.
Acid blend	1 tsp.	2 tsps.
Campden tablets	1	2
Yeast energizer		
or Vita-Vin	½ tsp.	½ tsp.
Wine yeast	1 package	1 package
Starting S.G. 1.095 to 1.100		

Note: You can, if you prefer, omit the raisins and substitute 10 fl. ozs. grape concentrate.

Salal Berry Wine

Ingredients	U.S. Measure	Canadian Measure
Salal berries	2 lbs.	3 lbs.
Raisins	½ lb.	½ lb.
Sugar	2½ lbs.	3 lbs.
Water	1 gal.	1 gal.
Acid blend	1 tsp.	2 tsps.
Campden tablets	1	2

Ingredients	U.S. Measure	Canadian Measure
Yeast nutrient	1 tsp.	1 tsp.
Wine yeast	1 package	1 package
Starting S.G. 1.095 to 1.100		

Note: You can, if you prefer, omit the raisins and substitute 10 fl. ozs. grape concentrate.

Saskatoon Berry Wine

Ingredients	U.S. Measure	Canadian Measure
Saskatoon berries	2½ lbs.	3 lbs.
Raisins	½ lb.	½ lb.
Sugar	2½ lbs.	3 lbs.
Water	1 gal.	1 gal.
Pectic enzyme	½ tsp.	½ tsp.
Acid blend	4 tsps.	5 tsps.
Campden tablets	1	2
Yeast energizer		
or Vita-Vin	½ tsp.	½ tsp.
Wine yeast	1 package	1 package
Starting S.G. 1.095 to 1.100		

Note: You can, if you prefer, omit the raisins and substitute 10 fl. ozs. red grape concentrate.

Thompson Seedless Grape Wine

This recipe makes 1 gallon of wine; you can multiply it according to the quantity you wish to make, or to the weight of grapes you have available.

Ingredients	U.S. Measure	Canadian Measure
Grapes	17 lbs.	20 lbs.
Sugar	4 ozs.	6 ozs.
Grape tannin	¼ tsp.	¼ tsp.
Acid blend	2 tsps.	3 tsps.
Campden tablets	1	2
Yeast nutrient	1 tsp.	1 tsp.
Wine yeast	1 package	1 package
Starting S.G. 1.085 to 1.090		

Method

Crush the grapes. Crush the Campden tablets and stir thoroughly into the crushed grapes. Press the grapes immediately to extract as much juice as possible. Then stir in the other ingredients and process as usual.

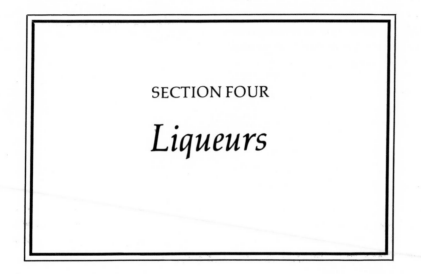

SECTION FOUR

Liqueurs

This section offers recipes and instructions for several liqueurs, all quick and easy to make. Store-bought liqueurs, of course, are produced by distillation; but for the home winemaker, that's illegal, so we use ready-distilled brandy or vodka. One noteworthy point: when buying the brandy or vodka, get the cheapest variety available – there's no point at all in using top-grade brands for this purpose. The same applies for the recipes that call for wine – if you are not using your own wine, then get a cheap variety. Don't think that this will spoil the finished liqueur; it won't.

THREE LIQUEURS FROM DRIED FRUITS

Processing methods are the same for all three. The dried fruit, for best results, should be fresh and soft to the touch, not completely dried out and hard. Use a light-coloured, clear, liquid honey; avoid any of the strong-flavoured varieties.

Apricot Liqueur

Ingredients

12 ozs. dried apricots	½ cup (4 fl. ozs.) honey
1¾ cups (14 ozs). white granulated sugar	40 fl. ozs. white wine
	8 fl. ozs. brandy

Peach Liqueur

Ingredients

16 ozs. dried peaches	½ cup (4 fl. ozs.) honey
1¾ cups (14 ozs.) white granulated sugar	40 fl. ozs. red wine
	8 fl. ozs. brandy

Prune Liqueur

Ingredients

16 ozs. dried prunes (remove stones)	½ cup (4 fl. ozs.) honey
1¾ cups (14 ozs.) white granulated sugar	40 fl. ozs. white wine
	8 fl. ozs. brandy

Method

Get a wide-mouth jar of the kind used for preserving fruits and vegetables, of about 80 fl. ozs. capacity.

Mix the sugar, honey and wine, stirring thoroughly to make sure of complete solution. Add the fruit, stir again, and cover with the lid of the preserving jar, or with sheet plastic tied down.

No fermentation lock is required, because there is no fermentation taking place; the alcohol already present is absorbing the flavour of the fruit. It does not matter, either, if there is a sizeable air space in the jar. Let it stand overnight at room temperature.

On the second day, stir in the brandy and cover again.

Stir once a day for a week; otherwise keep covered.

Let the jar stand for 3 more weeks at room temperature. The liqueur is now too syrupy to siphon, so pour it through a fine straining bag and bottle the clear liquid. It is ready to drink immediately.

A bonus: the remaining fruit is excellent for desserts. Store it in a covered jar in the refrigerator.

TWO LIQUEURS FROM FRESH FRUITS
Processing methods are the same for both.

Black Currant Liqueur (Cassis)

Ingredients

12 ozs. black currants	granulated sugar
2 cups (16 ozs.) white	26 fl. ozs. vodka

Cherry Liqueur

Ingredients

2 lbs. cherries	granulated sugar
2 cups (16 ozs.) white	26 fl. ozs. vodka

Method

Crush the fruit with a wooden spoon or stainless steel potato masher. (With the cherries, *don't* remove the stones.)

Mix the ingredients in a wide-mouth glass container. Close and seal tightly to reduce oxidation of the fruit.

Leave for 10 days at room temperature, or for 30 days in a refrigerator.

Strain through a filter bag or cloth; or, better still, use filter paper or a wine filter. The Cassis or Cherry Liqueur is ready to drink immediately.

Yield: 40 fl. ozs.

Note: The Cassis can be used to make a popular aperitif, similar to the French Kirr.

In an 8-oz. glass, mix:

1 fl. oz. Cassis

5 to 6 fl. ozs. well-chilled dry white wine (Chablis)

or Champagne (brut)

If you prefer it, you can also add ice; but that is not done in France.

Vanilla Vodka Liqueur

Ingredients

1 large vanilla bean	20 fl. ozs. water
4 cups (2 lbs.) white	20 fl. ozs. vodka
granulated sugar	2 ozs. instant coffee

Method

Cut the vanilla bean into pieces about ½ inch long.

Boil the water, dissolve the coffee and sugar, and add the cut-up vanilla bean.

Let it cool, then pour into a wide-mouth jar and add the vodka.

Stir once a day for a week; otherwise keep covered.

Let the jar stand 3 more weeks at room temperature. Strain and bottle the finished liqueur; it is ready to drink immediately.

SECTION FIVE

Second Wines

In *The Art of Making Wine* I discussed the technique of making second wine from pomace. Such second wine, inevitably, lacks some of the body and character of the first-run wine; but you can easily and economically upgrade it by the judicious use of grape concentrate. This technique has an added advantage: in many instances, you can get two or three different kinds of wine from the same batch of pomace.

Red Wine

You have made a batch of red wine from red California grapes. Then proceed as follows.

1 / Add to the unpressed pomace 1 gallon of water for each gallon of first-run wine you have removed.

2 / For each 12 U.S. gallons or 10 Canadian (imperial) gallons of water, add:

    160 ozs. Spanish Red Grape concentrate
    20 lbs. white granulated sugar
    3 ozs. acid blend
    1 oz. yeast nutrient

(The starting S.G. will be lower than you might expect – lower than for a comparable batch of first-run wine; but follow the directions, or you will get a sweet wine.)

3 / When S.G. falls to 1.010, rack into secondary fermentors, and from there on process like first-run wine.

White Wine

You have crushed, pressed and extracted the juice from a batch of white California grapes, to make first-run wine. Now, for your second-run wine, proceed as follows.

1 / Put the pressed grapes into a primary fermentor.

2 / For every 200 lbs. original weight of unpressed grapes, add:

    1 160-oz. can Spanish White Grape concentrate
    10 cans water
    16 lbs. white granulated sugar
    2 tsps. grape tannin
    4 ozs. acid blend
    10 Campden tablets
    1 oz. yeast nutrient
    Wine yeast

3 / Conduct the primary fermentation as usual. Stir, or punch down the cap, daily; but avoid excessive aeration.

4 / When S.G. falls to 1.020, rack into secondary fermentors and press the pomace. From there on, process like first-run wine.

White and Red Wine

Here's how to get white and red wine from the same batch of white California grapes. Crush and press the grapes to make first-run wine. Then proceed as follows.

1 / Put the pressed grapes into a primary fermentor.

2 / For every 200 lbs. original weight of unpressed grapes, add:

> 1 160-oz. can Spanish Red Grape concentrate
> 10 cans water
> 20 lbs. white granulated sugar
> 1 tsp. grape tannin
> 3 ozs. acid blend
> 10 Campden tablets
> 1 oz. yeast nutrient
> Wine yeast

3 / Conduct the primary fermentation as usual. Stir, or punch down the cap, daily.

4 / When S.G. falls to 1.020, rack into secondary fermentors and press the pomace. From there on, process like first-run wine.

> Now, from each 200 lbs. of fresh grapes, you have:
> 10-12 gals. first-run white wine,
> 10-12 gals. second-run red wine.

Rosé

You can divide your first-run white wine into two equal batches, and make one of them into a rosé. Process the first batch as usual for white wine. For each 6 gallons (U.S.) or 5 gallons (Canadian) in the second batch, add 1 28-oz. can California Red Grape concentrate; this will give you a very good rosé.

Now suppose you also use the previous recipe for red second wine; then, from each 200 lbs. white grapes you started with, you have:

> 5-6 gals. first-run white wine,
> 5-6 gals. first-run rosé,
> 10-12 gals. second-run red.

White, Rosé and Red

Here's how to get three different batches of wine, each 10-12 gallons, from 200 lbs. of white grapes. You have crushed, pressed and extracted the juice from your white grapes. For the second-run rosé proceed as follows.

1 / Put the pressed grapes into a primary fermentor.

2 / For every 200 lbs. original weight of unpressed grapes, add:

1 160-oz. can Spanish White Grape concentrate
2 28-oz. cans California Red Grape concentrate
10 160-oz. cans water
16 lbs. white granulated sugar
2 tsps. grape tannin
4 ozs. acid blend
10 Campden tablets
1 oz. yeast nutrient
Wine yeast

3 / Process in the same way as the other second-run wines. When S.G. falls to 1.020, rack into secondary fermentors, but do not press the pomace.

4 / Now for the third-run red wine. For every 200 lbs. original weight of unpressed grapes, add:

2 160-oz. cans Spanish Red Grape concentrate
10 cans water
4 lbs. white granulated sugar
2 tsps. grape tannin
2 ozs. acid blend
1 oz. yeast nutrient

5 / Conduct primary fermentation as usual. Stir, or punch down the cap, daily. When S.G. falls to 1.020, rack into secondary fermentors and press the pomace. Complete secondary fermentation as usual.

If you have a garden, you may as well dig in that pomace. It has yielded good service by producing:

10-12 gals. white wine,
10-12 gals. rosé,
10-12 gals. red wine

from each 200 lbs. of grapes, plus 3 160-oz. cans and 2 28-oz. cans of concentrate!

SECTION SIX

Fun and Frivolity
With Wine

Most of the time you will want to drink your wine just as it comes from the bottle, unmixed, undiluted, to enjoy the full flavour and aroma that you took such pains to produce. Yet there is a place for mixed drinks, using wine as a base – wine coolers, fruit-flavoured or herb-flavoured drinks, and so on.

One advantage of making coolers is that it cuts the alcohol content of the finished drink by half – down to 7%, 6% or less. So, at parties, people can take a fair amount of these drinks without getting inebriated.

The iced drinks are excellent for hot days, and the mulled wines are really warming in winter.

These mixed drinks, too, are an excellent use for a batch of wine – say a fruit wine – that is not quite up to snuff for serving as a table wine with food.

Here are some basic recipes. Try these first, then use your own ingenuity to create others on the same principles.

WINE COOLERS

Pour 4 fl. ozs. of any fruit wine – apricot, peach, blackberry, etc. – over ice cubes in a tumbler. Fill up with soda water (for a dry drink) or Seven Up (for a slightly sweet taste). Put a slice of cucumber at the side of the glass; or add a cherry, or a slice of orange, on a toothpick.

Sangria

Ingredients

1 26-oz. bottle red wine	Peel of 1 orange
2 fl. ozs. brandy	Peel of 1 lemon
4 tsps. white granulated sugar	Ice cubes to half-fill the container
1 cinnamon stick	10 fl. ozs. soda water

Method

Cut the orange and lemon peel in long, spiral strips. Mix all ingredients except the ice cubes and soda water, and put them in the refrigerator for 1 hour to leach the flavour. Just before serving, add the ice cubes and soda water.

Hard-Fruit Sangria

Ingredients

1 26-oz. bottle dry red wine	1 orange
½ cup white granulated sugar	1 pear
1 apple	1 7-oz. bottle soda water
1 lemon	Ice

Method

1 / Core the apple, but do not peel any of the fruit. Cut the fruit in large sections, place in a big bowl or pitcher, and sprinkle the sugar on it. Let it stand for at least 30 minutes. (The longer the fruit-sugar mixture stands, the stronger will be the flavour.)

2 / Add the wine and soda water; stir gently.

3 / Add the ice, in one large chunk — *not* in cubes, which melt too quickly, and tend to dilute the mixture.

4 / In serving, put a portion of fruit in each glass, and provide a pick so the fruit may be eaten — to some tastes, the best part!

May Bowle

This drink is traditionally made with woodruff, a shy herb with a star-white flower that imparts a fragrance like new-mown hay. Woodruff is not sold everywhere, but it is available if you care to search for it.

Ingredients

1 cup dried woodruff *or* 2 cups fresh woodruff	2 26-oz. bottles white wine
3 tbsps. white granulated sugar	1 cup (8 fl. ozs.) brandy
	1 26-oz. bottle champagne
	Rose petals
	Ice

Method

1 / Mix the sugar, woodruff and white wine; let them steep in the refrigerator overnight.

2 / Next day, shortly before serving, strain out the woodruff and pour the liquid over a chunk of ice, or a heap of ice cubes, in a chilled bowl. Add the brandy and stir in. (If you want extra strength, double the brandy to 2 cups.)

3 / At the last moment, in front of your guests, pour in the bottle of champagne, thoroughly chilled.

4 / Serve with a few rose petals in each glass. (Instead of rose petals, you can use a sprig of mignonette, or one of the tiny flower cups from a linden tree.)

Yield: about 20 servings, 4 fl. ozs. each.

Strawberry Bowle

Ingredients

2 cups fresh sliced strawberries	1 cup (8 fl. ozs.) brandy
3 tbsps. white granulated sugar	1 26-oz. bottle champagne
2 40-oz. bottles white wine	1 cup fresh whole strawberries
	Rose petals
	Ice

Method

1 / Mix the sliced strawberries, sugar and white wine; let them steep overnight in the refrigerator.

2 / Next day, shortly before serving, strain out the fruit. (You may find it has softened and darkened; but that's all right.) Pour the liquid over a chunk of ice or a heap of ice cubes in a chilled bowl. Add the brandy and stir in. (If you want extra strength, double the brandy to 2 cups.) Add the fresh whole berries.

3 / At the last moment, in front of your guests, pour in the bottle of champagne, thoroughly chilled.

4 / Serve with a few rose petals in each glass.

Yield: about 25 servings, 4 fl. ozs. each.

Peach Bowle and Pineapple Bowle

Proceed as with the Strawberry Bowle, substituting peaches or pineapple. Use the same quantities; but, for the fresh fruit served with the drinks, you obviously can't use whole peaches or pineapples, so cut them into convenient-sized pieces.

Mulled Wine

This is an excellent drink for wintertime. For each serving, take:

4 fl. ozs. any red wine
1 tsp. honey
1 fl. oz. apple juice

Heat the wine to 140°-150°F. – no more, or you will boil off all the alcohol.

Stir in the honey and apple juice, and serve in hot mugs.

You can make a wide variety of flavours for mulled wine. For example, instead of the apple juice, add a slice of orange and a cinnamon stick, or sprinkle a little nutmeg on the wine.

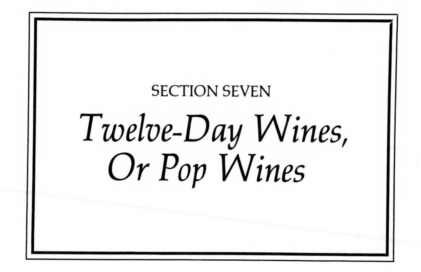

SECTION SEVEN

Twelve-Day Wines,
Or Pop Wines

By a pop wine I mean a sweet wine of low alcohol content (say 8% to 10%). An important feature of pop wine is that it contains a proportion of fresh, unfermented grape (or other fruit) juice: that's what gives it the rich fruit flavor that many people find so appealing–somewhat like a fresh fruit juice or punch.

General Procedure

1. With fruit concentrate of your choice, prepare a must of 1.075 S.G., holding back 30% of the concentrate under refrigeration, to be added at bottling time. For each gallon of must, add 1 teaspoon of Vita-Vin or any high-potency yeast nutrient. Adjust acid to .45% as tartaric. Ferment for 7 days in the primary fermentor.

2. Add Sparkolloid finings and rack into secondary fermentor, under fermentation locks. Three days is usually enough for the wine to finish fermenting. It should now be clear. The reason for fining at this stage is that the wine *must* be clear before filtration, otherwise the filter will get clogged.

3. Siphon back into primary fermentor; add the 30% of the concentrate that you reserved. Sweeten to taste with wine conditioner: about 2 ounces per gallon suits most tastes.

4. The next stage will be to filter the wine. After that process, the wine will be sterile; all the yeast will have been removed from it. Yet possibly, in the process of bottling, one or more bottles of the wine could become contaminated by airborne yeasts surviving in the environment from previous winemaking. Then those bottles of wine might start fermenting again. To avoid that risk, here's the procedure I recommend.

Using the Vinamat filter with "sterile" pads, filter the wine into gallon jugs. Into each gallon, after filtration, mix one teaspoon of the yeast inhibitor, potassium sorbate: that will guard against refermentation. This wine can be stored in the gallon jugs; or, if you prefer, it can be transferred to half-gallon jugs, or regular-size bottles. Whichever you choose, all jugs or bottles should previously be rinsed with a half-strength metabisulphite solution (1 ounce crystals per gallon of water). Fill bottles or jugs to within 2 inches of the top and apply corks or screw caps.

5. This wine is fit to drink after 24 hours' aging in the fridge; but it will be better if kept for a week. Most people prefer it served cold or on the rocks. Because of its low alcohol content, it will not keep more than 6, or at most 9 months. (If you want a wine that keeps well, use the traditional method.)

As for cost, at the time of writing, this type of wine works out at approximately 50 cents per bottle, for ingredients!

Now I will give a couple of recipes, and follow them with some notes on making your own recipes.

Spanish Grape

For this recipe, you can use white, red or rosé concentrate.

Ingredients

1 76-oz. (U.S.) or 80-oz. (imp.) can Spanish Grape Concentrate	9 tsps. acid blend
	2 tsps. yeast energizer
4 lbs. white granulated sugar	All-purpose wine yeast
9 cans water	*To be added later*
½ tsp. grape tannin	½ oz. Sparkolloid
	10 ozs. wine conditioner

Method

Reserve 27 ozs. of the concentrate, and conduct primary fermentation as usual.

Continue as described in the notes on General Procedure.

Filter wine with Vinamat, using two sterile pads for each 2½ U.S. gals. (2 imp. gals.) of wine. Alternatively, you can fine-filter the whole batch and then sterile-filter it with one set of sterile pads.

California Muscat

This will yield 12 26-oz. bottles of light, German-style wine. (I mention Muscat in the recipe, but the same formula can be used with almost any 26-28 oz. California grape concentrate, red or white.)

Ingredients

26 ozs. California Muscat Concentrate	½ tsp. grape tannin
	2 tsps. acid blend
18 ozs. white granulated sugar	2 tsps. yeast nutrient
	All-purpose wine yeast
2 gals. + 26 ozs. (U.S.) *or* 1 gal. + 134 ozs. (imp.) water	*To be added later*
	¼ oz. Sparkolloid
	4 ozs. wine conditioner

Method

Reserve 8 ozs. of the concentrate and conduct primary fermentation as usual.

Continue as described in notes on General Procedure.

Larger Quantities

To make 5 U.S. gals. from California concentrate, use 64 ozs. or ½ gal. of the concentrate; hold back 20 ozs. of it for bottling; use wine conditioner in the amount of 2 ozs. per gal.

You can make your own recipes from any single concentrate or blend of concentrates, following the guidelines laid down at #1 of General Procedune as to starting gravity, and reserving 30% of the concentrate; or you can adapt recipes in other parts of this book, modifying the quantity of concentrate accordingly.

I recommend using concentrates that contain no "gross lees", *i.e.* no bits of fruit or vegetable matter. Most good concentrates are filtered before being concentrated, therefore do not contain any such material. If gross lees are present, they will clog up the filter pads that we use to take out the yeast.

The process, as described above, includes fining of the wine; but if careful fining fails to clear a cloudy wine (or if you decide to experiment with fresh-fruit pop wines), then you can run the wine through the Vinamat filter twice. The first run, with coarse filter pads, will clear the wine; the second, with sterile pads, will remove the yeast.

Metric System

Before this book is out of print, some moves will have been made towards introduction of the metric system in North America. But the change-over will not be sudden. For some time, the old and new systems will overlap. Concentrates will be sold by quarts and litres; sugar will be packaged by pounds and kilograms; some bottles will be marked in fluid ounces, others in millilitres.

To ease you through this transition period, we print below some handy conversion tables, covering a range of weights, capacities and temperatures that will be useful for home winemaking.

Note that these tables do not pretend to be minutely exact; they give quantities to a degree of accuracy that you can expect to achieve, using spoons, cups, measuring-glasses, scales and thermometers in the home. For example, it would be absurd, for our purpose, to say that 1 teaspoon equals 4.929 millilitres; you aren't going to measure to a thousandth or a hundredth of a millilitre. So we say 1 teaspoon = 5 millilitres; that's close enough.

TEMPERATURE CONVERSION TABLE

Fahrenheit	Centigrade or Celsius	Fahrenheit	Centigrade or Celsius
32	0	86	30
41	5	95	35
50	10	104	40
59	15	113	45
68	20	122	50
77	25	131	55

WEIGHTS

U.S. and Canadian (imperial) weights are identical.

U.S. & Canadian to Metric

1 oz. = 28 grams	12 ozs. = ¾ lb. = 340 grams
2 ozs. = 57 grams	1 lb. = 454 grams
3 ozs. = 85 grams	2 lbs. = 907 grams
4 ozs. = ¼ lb. = 113 grams	5 lbs. = 2.268 kilograms
8 ozs. = ½ lb. = 227 grams	

Metric to U.S. & Canadian

1 gram = 1/30 oz.	500 grams = 1 lb. 1½ ozs.
10 grams = 1 dekagram = ⅓ oz.	750 grams = 1 lb. 10¼ ozs.
100 grams = 1 hectogram = 3½ ozs.	1000 grams = 1 kilogram = 2 lbs. 3 ozs.
250 grams = 8¾ ozs.	

FLUID MEASURE

U.S. and Canadian (imperial) fluid measure systems differ significantly; therefore we give two separate conversion tables.

U.S. to Metric

1 tsp. = 1/6 fl. oz. = 5 millilitres	1 cup = 8 fl. ozs. = 237 ml.
1 tbsp. = ½ fl. oz. = 15 ml.	1 fl. oz. = 29.5 ml.
	4 fl. ozs. = 118 ml.
8 fl. ozs. = 236 ml.	1 gal. = 8 pts. = 3.785 litres
12 fl. ozs. = 354 ml.	2 gals. = 7.57 litres
1 pint = 16 fl. ozs. = 473 ml.	5 gals. = 18.925 litres
26 fl. ozs. = 767 ml.	10 gals. = 37.85 litres
1 quart = 2 pints = 946 ml.	

Metric to U.S.

1 millilitre = 1 cubic centimeter = 1/5 tsp.	1 litre = 33.82 fl. ozs. = 1.057 quarts
5 ml. = 1 tsp.	2 litres = 2.114 qts.
10 ml. = 2 tsps.	5 litres = 1.32 gals.
1 deciliter = 100 ml. = 3.4 fl. ozs.	1 dekaliter = 2.64 gals.
750 ml. = 25.4 fl. ozs.	20 litres = 5.28 gals.

Canadian to Metric

1 tsp. = 1/6 fl. oz. = 5 millilitres*	1 pint = 20 fl. ozs. = 568 ml.
1 tbsp. = ½ fl. oz. = 15 ml.	26 fl. ozs. = 738 ml.
1 cup = 8.3 fl. ozs. = 237 ml.	1 quart = 1.136 litres
1 fl. oz. = 28 ml.	1 gal. = 4.546 litres
5 fl. ozs. = 142 ml.	5 gals. = 22.73 litres
10 fl. ozs. = 284 ml.	10 gals. = 45.46 litres
15 fl. ozs. = 426 ml.	

*The difference between the U.S. and Canadian systems is not large enough to affect teaspoon and tablespoon measurements; it becomes important when larger quantities are used.

Metric to Canadian	
1 millilitre = 1 cubic centimeter	750 ml. = 26.4 fl. ozs.
= 1/5 tsp.	1 litre = 35 fl. ozs. = 1.75 pints
5 ml. = 1 tsp.	5 litres = 1.1 gal.
10 ml. = 2 tsps.	1 dekaliter = 2.2 gals.
1 deciliter = 3.5 fl. ozs.	20 litres = 4.4 gals.

CONVERTING RECIPES

As the change-over to the metric system proceeds, we shall see more and more products packaged in metric-sized containers. Fon example, 30-ounce cans might be replaced by 1-litre cans, 15-oz. cans by ½-litre cans, 1-gallon bottles by 4- or 5-litre bottles, 2-lb. bags by 1-kilogram bags, and so on.

At present, obviously, we cannot predict every size of package that may come into production: but here are some hints for use when the old-style packages disappear from the market, so that you can continue to make up your favourite recipes.

Suppose, for example, you have a recipe of which the basic ingredients are 80 fl. ozs. (U.S.) red grape concentrate, 2 gals. (U.S.) water, and 1½ lbs. white sugar. (There will be other ingredients, of course, but let's consider just these, for simplicity.)

Suppose the 80-oz. cans of concentrate go off the market and are replaced by 1-litre cans. You want to make something near the same-sized batch of wine, so you buy 3 cans, 1 litre each, *i.e.* a total of 3 x 33.82 U.S. fl. ozs. = 101.46 U.S. fl. ozs.

You will probably want to use up all the concentrate on one batch of wine, rather than have some of it lying around. So you are now going to work with 101.46 fl. ozs. of concentrate instead of 80 fl. ozs; that's an increase of 21.46 fl. ozs.

For convenient calculation, convert this to a percentage.

$$\frac{21.46 \times 100}{80} = \text{approximately } 27\%$$

That percentage figure is the main one you need; simply apply it to the other major ingredients of the recipe.

Water: 2 gals. + 27% = a little over 2½ gals (U.S.)
= 9.5 liters (approx.)

Sugar: 1½ lbs. + 27% = 1 lb. 14½ ozs. (approx.)
= 865 grams

Other measured ingredients would be similarly increased by 27%. As a check on your calculations, take particular care to read the starting specific gravity, and correct it if necessary by adding sugar or water. Make a note of your calculations, so that you have them available for future use.

Just one more example. Suppose you are going to make mead from a recipe that calls for 3 lbs. of honey, but you find honey is now being sold by the kiogram. So you get 2 kg., *i.e.* 4.4 lbs. That is an increase of 1.4 lbs. over the amount prescribed by the recipe.

Calculate the percentage increase:

$$\frac{1.4 \times 100}{3} = 47\% \text{ (approx.)}$$

The original recipe called for 50 fl. ozs. fresh orange juice, so you increase that quantity, too, by 47%.

$$50 + 47\% = 73 \text{ fl. ozs. (U.S.)}$$
$$= 2.153 \text{ litres}$$

The original recipe says "Warm water to 1 gal."; so you substitute "Warm water to 1.47 gals." = 5.564 litres.

It's all a little extra fun, added to the ordinary pleasure of winemaking. (And if you're no whiz at arithmetic, you can always use a calculating machine!)

Index

Acid: *blends*, 3; *content*, 4; *in fruit*, 7; *testing*, 5-7
Additives, 7-11
Alcohol: *content in wine*, 12-16; *yield*, 57-58
Ammonium sulphate, 8
Antioxidants, 14-16; *for bottling*, 17
Apricot: *dessert wine recipe*, 80; *liqueur recipe*, 101

Banana wine recipe, 88-89
Bardolino recipe, 68
Barrel aging, 16
Beet wine recipe, 89
Birch sap wine recipe, 89
Black currant liqueur recipe, 102
Blackberry dessert wine recipe, 80-81
Bottling, 17-18
Burgandy recipe, 68-69

California muscat pop wine recipe, 114
Carrot wine recipe, 90
Cassis recipe, 102
Citrus champagne recipe, 90
Chablis recipe, 69
Cherry: *dessert wine recipe*, 81; *liqueur recipe*, 102
Citric acid, 3
Claret recipe, 69-70
Cleaning, 18
Closures, 18-20
Concentrates, 20-25; *blending*, 23-25; *colour*, 21; *cost*, 20-21; *red*, 22; *white*, 22
Copper sulphate, 9
Corking machines, 19-20
Corks, 18-19
Cream sherry recipe, 70
Country wines basic formula, 25-26

East India sherry recipe, 73-74
Elderberry wine recipes, 81-82, 91

Fermentation locks, 26
Filtering, 26-33
Filters: *Fessler*, 30; *Grey Owl*, 27-28; *Harris*, 28; *Vinamat*, 30-33; *Vinbright*, 29-30
Fresh fig wine recipe, 91
Fruit wines: *acid content*, 4; *tropical*, 63

Gooseberry: *champagne recipe*, 83; *wine recipe*, 82
Grape tannin, 8
Grapes: *growing*, 37; *hybrid*, 35-37; *red*, 34-35; *white*, 35; *vinifera*, 37-38
Grapefruit wine recipe, 91-92
Graves recipe, 71

Lactic acid, 3
Liebfraumilch recipe, 83

Magnesium sulphate, 8
Marsala recipe, 71-72
May bowle recipe, 110
Mead recipes, 92-93
Measurements, 50
Melomel recipe, 92
Metabisulphite, 10-11
Metric system, 117-20
Moselle recipe, 72-73
Mountain ash wine recipe, 97-98
Mulberry wine recipe, 93
Mulled wine recipe, 111
Mustix, 6-7

Old brown sherry recipe, 73-74
Oregon grape wine recipe, 93-94

Parsley wine recipe, 94
Parsnip wine recipe, 94-95
Passionfruit wine recipe, 84
Pasteurization, 61-63
Peach: *bowle recipe*, 111; *dessert wine recipe*, 84-85; *liqueur recipe*, 101
Pectic enzyme, 8
Pineapple: *bowle recipe*, 111; *wine recipe*, 95
Plastic containers, 50-51
Plum dessert wine recipe, 85
Pop wines: *acid content*, 4; *creating recipes*, 115; *procedure*, 113
Prune liqueur recipe, 101
Pumpkin wine recipe, 95
Pyment recipe, 93

Quince wine recipe, 96
Quinine-flavoured aperitif recipe, 74-75

Red currant wine recipe, 96
Refractometer, 12-14
Rice wine recipe, 96-97
Rose: *hip wine recipe*, 97; *petal wine recipe*, 97
Rowanberry wine recipe, 97-98
Ruby port recipe, 75-76

Saki recipe, 96-97
Salal berry wine recipe, 98
Sangria recipe, 109; *hard-fruit recipe*, 109-10
Saskatoon berry wine recipe, 98-99
Sauterne recipe, 76
Second wine recipes, 105-7
Sodium erythorbate, 8, 15-16
Spanish grape pop wine recipe, 114
Sparkling pash recipe, 85-86
Sparkling rosé recipe, 77

Sparkling wine: *deep-freeze method,*
    54-55; *soda-siphon method,* 54
Sterilants, 55-56
Strawberry bowle recipe, 110-111
Succinic acid, 3
Sugar: *and alcohol yield,* 57-58;
    berry, 56; *candy,* 56; *dextrose,* 56;
    dark sugars, 56; *in wines,* 7; *and*
    specific gravity, 58; *sucrose,* 56
Sulphur dioxide: *as antioxidant,* 15;
    as sterilant, 9-11; *control,* 58-61
Sweet mead recipe, 93

Tablets, 63
Tarragona port recipe, 77-78
Tartaric acid, 4
Thompson seedless grape wine
    recipe, 99
Tritton, Mrs. S.M., 2

Urea, 8

Vanilla vodka liqueur recipe, 103

Wagner, Philip, 2, 5
Wine: *defined,* 2; *judging,* 42-50;
    nutriment, 11-12; *serving,* 51-54
Wine conditioner, 63-64
Winery, home: *construction,* 38-39;
    equipment, 40-41; *operation,* 41-42

Yeast energizer, 7-8
Yeast nutrient, 8